WORD ORDER PATTERNING
IN MIDDLE ENGLISH

JANUA LINGUARUM

STUDIA MEMORIAE
NICOLAI VAN WIJK DEDICATA

edenda curat

CORNELIS H. VAN SCHOONEVELD
STANFORD UNIVERSITY

NR. XIX

1962
MOUTON & CO. · 'S-GRAVENHAGE

WORD ORDER PATTERNING

IN

MIDDLE ENGLISH

A QUANTITATIVE STUDY
BASED ON PIERS PLOWMAN AND MIDDLE
ENGLISH SERMONS

by

WALERIAN ŚWIECZKOWSKI

LUBLIN

1962

MOUTON & CO. · 'S-GRAVENHAGE

Printed in The Netherlands by Mouton & Co., Printers, The Hague.

TABLE OF CONTENTS

0. INTRODUCTION

0.1   "The rules of word-position have too long been the Cinderella of linguistic science – how many even of the best grammars are wholly or almost wholly silent about them! . . . And although in English a change of word-order will in many cases completely alter the meaning of the proposition, this subject is, in most grammars, treated inadequately, if at all." [1] This statement is nearly as true today as it was more than sixty years ago, when it was first made. The first decades of the twentieth century produced a certain number of serious studies of the subject, but these pioneer works are of necessity limited in scope. [2] Since the 1930-s only a handful of scholars have approached the problem of word order systematically, but these works do not differ in any essential way from their predecessors. The advantage of a series of studies, in which the same methods are applied to various texts, is obvious. For this reason it had been thought proper to follow the traditional lines where possible.

0.1.1   At least some of the limitations of well established methods, it is hoped, are compensated by the procedure adopted in the present study. The main innovation, namely the introduction of the O1 notations, which provides the key to all the problems selected for the analysis, does not on the one hand have the disadvantage of inapplicability of the present results to those obtained in previous works, and on the other seems to offer treatment to problems which had previously puzzled many writers.

[1]   Jespersen, O., *Progress in Language* (New York, 1894).
[2]   Only the subject-predicate relations received satisfactory treatment, while the arrangement of other elements in the sequence had been dealt with in a fragmentary way. About the position of the object, for instance, there is an almost complete silence.

"To take one of those problems:", writes Jespersen, "What is the reason of the prevalence of the word-order – subject-verb-object – in English, Danish, French, Chinese, to mention only a very small number of languages? The fact of "that heathen Chinee" using the same order as ourselves precludes the supposition, often resorted in such cases, that one of the European nations has borrowed the usage from one of the others, and shows the phenomenon to be founded in the very nature of human thought, though its non-prevalence in most of the older Arian languages goes far to show that this particular order is only natural to developed human thought." [3] The suggested answer assumes too many things, but it is probably partly true. The more archaic a language, the newer the words, the greater the amount of information they convey. As time goes on, the frequency of some words increases at the expense of others, with a simultaneous decrease in their amount of information. This fact is stressed by Henry Sweet, who wrote: "All words that express new ideas are more or less emphatic; while words that express ideas already familiar or that can be taken for granted are unemphatic." [4] Unemphatic words often lose their original meaning and become part of the grammatical structure of the language. These grammatical words tend to become so frequent that "meaningful" words are found surrounded by the "empty" words. Characteristic patterns, hereafter called semantic load patterns, thus result. These patterns, which naturally differ from language to language, may be regarded, at least in part, as accounting for the various word order patterns. That this is so in the case of Middle English, will be shown in the following pages.

Jespersen may be again used for providing a concrete example. On the pages of the same *Progress in Language* the following difficulty is presented: "In Old English prose the subject is already placed before the verb in nearly every sentence; the exceptions are almost the same as in Modern German or Danish; thus inversion is the rule after adverbs such as *pā* (while, curi-

[3] Jespersen, *op. cit.*, p. 64.
[4] Sweet, H., *A Primer of Spoken English* (Oxford, 1890).

ously enough, the subject precedes the verb where the clause is introduced by *hwæt pā* or *efne pā*)." The present paper suggests a solution of problems of this kind by an attempt to establish the relations between word order and semantic load patterns.

0.1.2 These patterns, symbolized in the 01 notations, also make possible a simpler description of the various types of word order hitherto offered, and also their number can be reduced. Thus, for instance, Andrew [5] distinguishes three different kinds of order for Old English: Common order, conjunctive order and demonstrative order, the difference consisting in the presence or absence of a conjunction or a demonstrative pronoun. The two, however, have one thing in common: the absence of lexical meaning, and this feature they will be found to share with a number of subjects and predicates. If the absence of lexical meaning is symbolized by 0, and its presence by 1, the three types can be described in a simpler way: by means of two variables only, namely the word order and the semantic load pattern. It will be seen that Middle English word order can be handled in the same way.

0.2 Middle English texts present nothing like the rigorous word order of present day English. Relative freedom, however, does not preclude the presence of general rules, nor the prevalence of one particular pattern or type of pattern. The present study aims at establishing what is typical.

It may be objected that the choice of texts, on which the analysis is based, promises but few chances for achieving this aim. Although it is granted that poetry can distort "normal" word order, and the differences between *Piers Plowman* and the *Middle English Sermons,* as will be seen, are considerable, the texts have nevertheless striking features in common, which permit

---

[5]   Andrew, S. O., "Some Principles of Old English Wordorder", *Medium Aevum,* III (1934); *Syntax and Style in Old English* (Cambridge, 1940), p. 1.

some generalizations. The second answer to the possible objection is based on the results of many students of word order. The statistics, whether of prose or poetry, are very similar for various texts of a given historical epoch. "A study of prose and verse usage", Andrews writes in reference to Old English, "leeds to the conclusion that the same rules hold for verse as for prose both in syntax and word order." [6]

There is a very definite advantage in basing a study of this kind on texts so different in nature, for the larger the difference between the texts, the greater the chances that peculiarities of special types of writing will not be identified as features of the language. "... Just as we must forget, for a little while at least, that humans have widely different individualities if we wish to study them in the mass, so we must forget that literary works are highly individual creations if we wish to realize what they have in common, in spite of all their differences." [7]

0.3   The present survey is a study of the problem of word order "in the mass". Strictly speaking, no such thing like normal word order exists, since every text shows characteristics which it does not share with others. Sometimes isolated sentences, as proverbial expressions, are recommended as most "normal", [8] but they also refer to a context which can affect the order of words. Even in languages where word order has a distinctive function there are exceptions to rules often with redundant features indicating a syntactical function normally expressed by order. This being the situation, word order can hardly be dealt with otherwise than in great numbers.

The present study is strictly quantitative in character with all the conclusions based on numerical data.

---

[6]   Andrew, S. O., *Syntax and Style in Old English*, Preface.
[7]   Herdan, G., *Language as Choice and Chance* (Groningen, 1956), p. 2.
[8]   For instance Zenon Klemensiewicz, "Lokalizacja podmiotu i orzeczenia w zdaniach izolowanych", *Biuletyn Polskiego Tow. Jezyk.*, IX (1949), pp. 8-19.

0.4   A result of a quantitative survey of this kind is the fact that products of wilful creation appear simply as variants of the typical expenditure of linguistic material. This enforces limitations, of which the writer is fully aware. There is no doubt, for instance, that the requirements of metre (in the case of *Piers Plowman*) will modify the typical order, and it would be of great interest to establish how far this influence goes. Unfortunately neither does the scope of this thesis, nor the methods employed allow such a broad treatment.

Another limitation is dictated by the fact that the sentence is here treated as the largest unit of structure. The arrangement of elements possibly due to the preceding sentence received treatment only in so far, as this is reflected in the occurrence of substitutes. Also all considerations of style, such as emphasis, symmetry and asymmetry, embellishments etc., will be excluded from the study in spite of their importance in the word order problem.

These and other limitations, however, do not seem to impair the general argument of the present work, since their inclusion into the study would rather amplify our knowledge of the particular texts, than provide general characteristics of word order patterning in Middle English.

0.4.1   In the course of history English word order developed a distinctive function only in the case of the subject-predicate-object arrangement. Other members of the sentence, though having their habitual position, are elements of redundancy, and as such allow a certain margin of freedom which gives opportunity for individual style.[9] For this reason only subject-predicate-object relations will be studied here.

0.5   Previous studies of the problem of word order have already been mentioned (paragraph 0.1) and a list of titles is included in the Bibliography. None of these works covers the problem of word order in *Piers Plowman* or the *Middle English Sermons,*

[9]   Sapir, E., *Language* (New York), p. 37.

and only a few authors gave a passing notice to the position of the object in the sentence, while the majority concentrated on subject-predicate relations only, or on the position of modifiers.

0.6 Chapter 1 of the present study analyses the subject-predicate relations, Chapter 2 the relation of the predicate to other elements in the clause, Chapter 3 the position of the object. Each of these chapters falls into two parts, the first being devoted to *Piers Plowman,* the second to *Middle English Sermons.* In Chapter 4 numerical data from various sources are cited, and the results of the present analysis are compared with those of other studies.

0.7 Most of the terms to be used throughout the paper are those ordinarily employed in similar studies and need no special definitions. In a few cases, however, terms have been decided upon for a particular purpose. Thus *semantic load* refers to the presence or absence of lexical meaning in a word: words that have only a grammatical function (e.g., substitutes, auxiliaries, conjunctions) are semantically light, while those that have a lexical meaning as well as a grammatical one are heavy. If Fx means "has lexical meaning", Gx "is heavy" and Hx "is light", the definition can be expressed in the following way:

$$(x)\ (Fx)\ Gx \cdot - Fx\ Hx)$$

Semantic load patterns are groupings of light and heavy words in any characteristic arrangement that is repeated.

The second term that calls for a definition is *prepositional,* which is any word (or words) belonging to the associative group of the predicate, but the predicate itself, which stands at the beginning of a sentence or clause. If P_1, P_2 ... P_n stands for any member of the associative group of the predicate, and P_a for the predicate itself, and if Fx means "stands first in the clause", the following formula will express the definition:

$$(x)\ (x\ E\ P_1, P_2, \ldots P_n) \cdot - (x \equiv P_a) \cdot Fx$$

0.8 References are made to the Text (version), the Passus and the line in the case of *Piers Plowman,* in the case of the *Middle English Sermons* to the page (ed. Woodburn O. Ross, London, Oxford University Press, 1940) and the line. Thus C, XIII, 25 means *Piers Plowman,* Text C, Passus XIII, line 25; and 143,30 means *Middle English Sermons,* page 143, line 30.

1. THE POSITION OF SUBJECT AND PREDICATE IN RELATION TO ONE ANOTHER

1.1 *PIERS PLOWMAN*

1.1.1　In the problem of order of elements only clauses with an EXPRESSED subject and predicate are of any value. The number of such clauses in the three texts of *Piers Plowman* amounts to 1332 in Text A, 2967 in Text B and 3336 in Text C (7635 in all). In a considerable number of clauses, where two or more subjects refer to one and the same predicate (e.g. *Curatours, that schulden kepe hem clene of heore bodies, thei beoth cumbred in care* A, I, 169),[1] only the subject which is nearest to the predicate is taken into consideration.

There is no concentration in the distribution of either the subject-predicate or the predicate-subject order in any part of the examined texts, but the former pattern is found more frequently than the latter, the proportions being 1004 to 328 for Text A, 2279 to 688 for Text B and 2607 to 729 for Text C.

Table I

	SUBJECT-PREDICATE	PREDICATE-SUBJECT
Text A	75.5% (1004)	24.5% (328)
Text B	76.8% (2279)	23.2% (688)
Text C	78.7% (2607)	21.3% (729)
Texts A, B, C	77.6% (7527)	22.4% (1745)

---

[1]　In quotations from the analysed texts, ð and ȝ spellings appear as *th* and *g*.

Examples:

Subject-predicate order:

> *Seruauns for heore seruise . . . taketh mede of heore*
> *maystres* A, III, 210;
> *Ther heo is wel with the king* A. III, 148;
> *I hailsed hem hendely* B. VIIII, 10;
> *Ac Conscience kwew hem wel* C, V, 32.

Predicate-subject order:

> *Dredeles is Dobet A*, XII, 191;
> *And thanne gan alle the comune crye* B, P, 143;
> *So of hol herte cometh hope* C, IV, 354;
> *Schal never mon uppon molde meytene the leste* A, II,
> 171.

1.1.2 Even by eye can one detect that the predicate-subject order is found far more frequently in sequences which begin with an element (or elements) not belonging to the associative group of the subject,[2] that is, by any form of a verbal modifier, an object (direct or indirect), or a dependent clause. The term prepositional element, or prepositional[3] may be conveniently used for the purpose of discussion.

An analysis of the texts reveals the following figures: The 1332 subjects in Text A are preceded by a prepositional in 576 cases, which constitutes 43.6% of the total. The analogous numbers for Texts B and C are: 1848 clauses without a prepositional against 1119 clauses with a prepositional in the former, 2033 against 1303 in the latter, which constitutes 37.7% and 38.3% of the respective totals. However, despite the fact that this type of structure includes less than a half of the whole body of the given texts, it is there that practically all the instances of predicate-subject order are found. The contingency tables below show the distribution of the two patterns in relation to the presence or absence of prepositionals.

---

[2] The notion of associative groups is taken from Rulon S. Wells, "Immediate Constituents", *Language*, XXIII (1947), p. 90.
[3] Not to be confused with the term as used by Trager and Smith, *An Outline of English Structure* (Norman, Oklahoma, 1951).

Table II

Text A

	NO PREPOSITIONAL	PREPOSITIONAL	
SP	728 (569)	276 (435)	1004
PS	28 (187)	300 (142)	328
	756	576	1332

Table III

Text B

	NO PREPOSITIONAL	PREPOSITIONAL	
SP	1726 (142)	553 (733)	2279
PS	122 (429)	566 (247)	688
	1848	1119	2967

Table IV

Text C

	NO PREPOSITIONAL	PREPOSITIONAL	
SP	1929 (161)	678 (880)	2607
PS	104 (382)	625 (231)	729
	2033	1303	3336

The discrepancies between the actual cell values and the expected values are large enough to claim that the dependence of the prepositional is very strong. The application of the formula for the coefficient of contingency [4] will make it possible to find how the degree of association between the two variables fluctuates in the three texts of *Piers Plowman*.

From the figures it follows that the dependence of subject-predicate relations on the presence of the prepositional is high, and this encourages further investigation of the problem.

---

[4]   The formula and its application is fully described by S. Siegel, *Non-Parametric Statistics for Behavioral Sciences* (New York, 1956), p. 196 ff.

$$C = \sqrt{\frac{x^2}{N + x^2}}$$

$$x^2 = \sum_{i-1}^{r} \sum_{j-1}^{k} \frac{(Oij - Eij)^2}{Eij}$$

Table V [5]

	TEXT A	TEXT B	TEXT C
x^2	403.0	2 433.2	3047.4
N	1332	2967	3336
C	0.57	0.91	0.91

Tables VI—VIII is a graphic representation of the distribution of the two patterns in question within the two types of sentences.

Examples:

> *Subject-predicate, no prepositional:*
> > *And Concience com aftur* A, VIII, 120;
> > *The pope and alle the prelates presentz vnderfongen* B, III, 214;
> > *Mercy is a mayde there* C, VIII, 288.

[5] Text A:

$$x^2 = \frac{(728 - 569)^2}{569} + \frac{(276 - 435)^2}{435} + \frac{(28 - 187)^2}{187} + \frac{(300 - 142)^2}{142} = 430.0$$

$$C = \sqrt{\frac{430.0^2}{1332 + 430.0^2}} = 0.572$$

Text B:

$$x^2 = \frac{(1726 - 142)^2}{142} + \frac{(553 - 733)^2}{733} + \frac{(122 - 429)^2}{429} + \frac{(566 - 247)^2}{247} = 2433,2$$

$$C = \sqrt{\frac{2433.2^2}{2967 + 2433.2^2}} = 0.905$$

Text C:

$$x^2 = \frac{(1929 - 161)^2}{161} + \frac{(678 - 880)^2}{800} + \frac{(625 - 231)^2}{231} + \frac{(104 - 328)^2}{328} = 3047.4$$

$$C = \sqrt{\frac{3047.4^2}{3336 + 3047.4^2}} = 0.914$$

Table VI

Text A

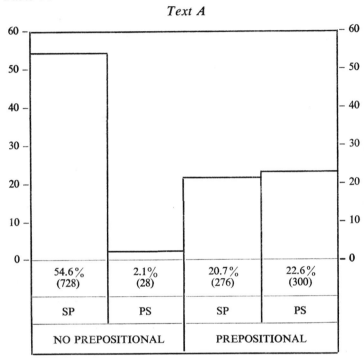

54.6% (728)	2.1% (28)	20.7% (276)	22.6% (300)
SP	PS	SP	PS
NO PREPOSITIONAL		PREPOSITIONAL	

Predicate-subject, no prepositional:
 And arn none for sothe . . . as thise A, IX, 283;
 For wit ge neuere who is worthi B, VII, 78;
 Ys no final loue with this folke C, IX, 216.
Subject-predicate, with prepositional:
 Lo! logyk I lered hire A, II, 127;
 Wel thow wost B, III, 179;
 And yf he wratthe, we mowe be war C, I, 189.
Predicate-subject, with prepositional:
 Thus 1-robed in russet romed I a-boute A,IX, 1;
 "By a forbisene," quod the frere B, VIII, 29;
 In glotenye . . . goth they to bedde C, I, 44.

It is remarkable that, although non-prepositional clauses out-number prepositional ones, the former sequences contain between only one tenth and one sixth of the predicate-subject patterns,

Table VII

Text B

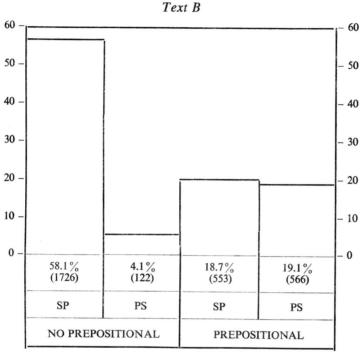

58.1% (1726)	4.1% (122)	18.7% (553)	19.1% (566)
SP	PS	SP	PS
NO PREPOSITIONAL		PREPOSITIONAL	

while the less frequent prepositional clauses include the rest.

This striking proportion cannot be without significance and will therefore be dealt with at length.

1.1.3   As has been remarked above, the SP pattern occurs about three times more frequently than the PS pattern and may therefore be regarded as the typical pattern for the text of *Piers Plowman*. The reverse order, however, is found often enough not to permit the application of the term "exceptional", and may therefore be treated as a sub-pattern.

Section 1.1.2 indicates the distribution of the typical pattern in the two types of sentence structures. An effort will be made to establish what correlations, and to what degree, there exist between the two word order patterns and other elements con-

Table VIII

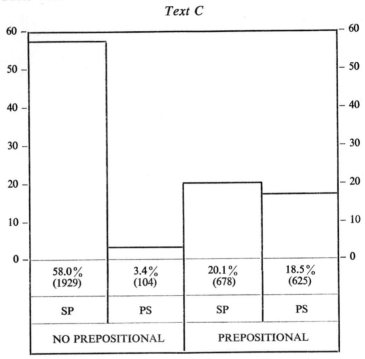

Text C

58.0% (1929)	3.4% (104)	20.1% (678)	18.5% (625)
SP	PS	SP	PS
NO PREPOSITIONAL		PREPOSITIONAL	

stituting a given sequence. Since the occurrence of PS in sentences with no prepositionals is close to exceptional, it is convenient to start the analysis with sentences where the pattern occurs more often.

Sentences with a prepositional have been defined (1.1.2) as sequences which begin with an element not belonging to the associate group of the subject; this element, then, either belongs to the associative group of the verb, or is more or less closely connected with it (a predicative or an object, for instance, is more closely related to the predicate than are verbal modifiers). On the basis of the assumption that syntactically related elements have a tendency to form continuous word groups in the sequence, the following hypothesis is proposed: If a syntactic unit belonging to the associative group of the verb precedes the subject in the sequence, the order of the predicate in relation to its subject is statistically predictable, the degree of determinancy being higher the closer the connection of the prepositional with the predicate. The following section is an attempt to test this hypothesis.

1.1.4   In order to find to what extent the presence of a prepositional determines the occurrence of either the SP or the PS pattern, all the given sentences have been classed according to the character of their prepositionals, that is, according to the functions they perform in the sentence.[6] The distribution of the respective patterns was indeed found to be different in the various groups, as shown in the following table. (Figures in brackets indicate the total number of cases of a given prepositional.)

Table IX

CHARACTER OF PREPOSITIONAL.	PERCENTAGE OP PS		
	TEXT A	TEXT B	TEXT C
1. Predicative	63.3 (19)	100 (23)	100 (13)
2. Object	63.7 (209)	69.7 (453)	61.0 (514)
3. Adverb of place	57.4 (54)	47.0 (83)	52.9 (127)
4. Adverb of time	54.6 (128)	48.7 (236)	52.6 (266)
5. Adverb of manner	42.0 (100)	37.3 (112)	42.7 (185)
6. Other	18.5 (65)	14.3 (217)	0.8 (189)

[6]   A few sentences, where it was impossible the decide whether they do or do not posses a prepositional, have not been taken into account in this study. Examples: *And alle that of that Caym come, Christ hem hatede aftur* A,X,146 (where the direct object is mentioned twice and placed before and after the subject); *Preestes and other peple to Peers thei drowen* C,IX,190 (where *to Peers*, the possible propositional, is put between a subject which is mentioned twice).

The six categories of prepositionals can easily be grouped into three classes (1.2– 3,4,5 – 6) differing in the degree of close relationship to the predicates in the given sequences, the first being very closely linked with the predicate, the last very loosely, the adverbial modifiers occupying a medium position.

The following table is a graphic representation of the correlation between the two variables: the occurrence of predicate-subject patterns and the character of the prepositional in the given sentence. ...... is used for Text A, - - - - for Text B and - . - . - . - for Text C.

Table X

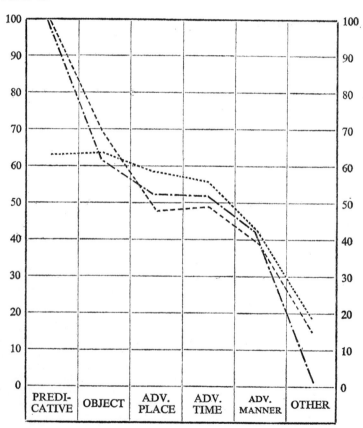

The curve shows how gradually the number of PS patterns decreases with the decrease in closeness of relationship of the given prepositionals to the predicates, the points for each text being within the limits of about ten per cent for each class of prepositional. The only disturbing feature is the distance between the points of Texts B and C from that of Text A in the class of predicatives. This may be partly due to the fact that predicatives occur comparatively rarely as prepositional (19, 23, 13 cases), which leaves room for accidental relations. Moreover, it was sometimes impossible to identify a noun in the function of a predicative. In doubtful cases (and where possible) the noun preceding the predicate was interpreted as a subject (since the subject-predicate order is the typical one), the noun following the predicate as a predicative.

Examples:
1. *The prepositional is a predicative:*
    PS: *Worthi is the werkmon his hure to haus* A, 11, 91;
    Ne rygte sori for my cynnes get was I neuere B, V, 406;
    Bygute was he neuere C, III, 144.
    SP: *Holi churche icham* A, I, 73;
    No occurrence in Texts B and C)
2. *The prepositional is an object:*
    PS: *The culorum of this clause kepe I not to schewe* A, III, 264;
    "What! awake, renke!" quod Repentance B, V, 399;
    And that seeth the saule C, II, 39.
    SP: *Caro hit hette* A, X, 38;
    This I trowe B, I, 143;
    Bothe wyndowes and wowes ich wolle amenden C, IV, 65.
3. *The prepositional is an adverb of place:*
    PS: *Ther prechede a pardoner* A, P, 65;
    Therinne wonieth a wighte B, I, 63;
    Ther was no lad that lyuede C, IX, 194.
    SP: *And atte newe feire he leyede hire to sulle* A, V, 171;
    And in the stories he techeth to bistowe B, VII, 75;
    Preastes and other peple to Pers thei drowen C, IX, 190.
4. *The prepositional is an adverb of time:*
    PS: *And thanne cam Coueytise* B, V, 188;

       Thanne laughten thei leue . . . at meede **A, III, 26;**
       Thanne sayde Symonye that . . . **C, III, 74.**
  SP: *And aftur mony metes his mawe is a-longet* **A, VII, 254;**
       Thanne Conscience vppon his calpe karieth forth faste
       B, IV, 23;
       And sitthe he preide prelates and prestes to-geders
       C, VI, 141.
 5. *The prepositional is an adverb of manner:*
  PS: *And so cometh Dobest aboute* **A, X, 212;**
       For thus bid the gospel **B, III, 75;**
       As wroth as the wynd wex Nede ther—after **C, IV, 486.**
  SP: *So steornelice he lokede* **A, VII, 305;**
       Curteisliche the kynge thanne come agein Resoun **B, IV,**
       44;
     For wel ge witen . . . that . . . **C, III, 142.**
 6. *The prepositional is represented by any other word(s):*
  PS: *Of other heuene . . . holde thei no tale* **A, I, 9;**
       For hunger or for thurst shal neuere fisshe . . . defien my
       wombe **B, V, 389;**
       Wist I this for sothe, shulde I neuere forthere a fote . . .
       C, V, 642.

1.1.5 The correlation between the two word order patterns and the character of the prepositional, though statistically constant, is not detectable in all cases; moreover, PS patterns occur, though less frequently, in sequences without a prepositional. In order to find what other factors coincide with the SP *versus* PS occurrences, SP and PS sequences which lack a prepositional will be examined below.

An analysis of the two elements that constitute the subject-predicate pattern itself revealed marked characteristic features which throw more light on the mechanism of the SP and PS interplay.

In a number of very clear cases, where all the syntactic constituents were identical and the only difference lay in the use of a nominal subject and a full verb in the function of the predicate on the one hand and the use of a pronominal subject and an auxiliary (or the copulative) in the function of the predicate on the other, it seemed evident that the choice of either the SP or the PS pattern depended to a large degree exactly on these differences in the character of subject and predicate. The criterion for detecting these differences is what can be called SEMANTIC LOAD: the opposition will consist in the presence or absence of this semantic load. Pronouns, auxiliary verbs and the copulative will be regarded as units having only a grammatical, but no lexical function, nouns and full verbs as having both functions. Symbols used: S: nominal subject; s: proniminal subject; P: full verb as predicate; p: auxiliary verb or copulative as predicate. The result of the analysis presents the following picture:

Table XI   *Text A*

SP	98.4% (186)	PS	1.6% (3)	total: 189
sP	97.2% (205)	Ps	2.8% (6)	total: 211
Sp	90.0% (130)	pS	10.0% (13)	total: 143
sP	97.8% (207)	ps	2.2% (6)	total: 213

Table XII   *Text B*

SP	95.0% (474)	Ps	5.0% (26)	total: 500
sP	97.7% (459)	Ps	2.3% (11)	total 470
Sp	82.6% (256)	pS	17.4% (56)	total 321
sP	94.8% (528)	ps	5.2% (29)	total: 557

Table XIII   *Text C*

SP	97.5% (509)	PS	2.5% (13)	total: 522
sP	97.7% (464)	Ps	2.3% (11)	total: 475
Sp	88.8% (333)	pS	11.2% (42)	total: 375
sp	94.2% (623)	ps	5.8% (38)	total: 661

When the percentages within the predicate-subject group itself are compared, the result is the following:

Table XIV

TEXT A	TEXT B	TEXT C
PS 10.7%	PS 21.6%	PS 12.6%
Ps 21.2%	Ps 9.0%	Ps 10.8%
pS 46.7%	pS 45.8%	pS 40.2%
ps 21.3%	ps 23.6%	ps 36.4%

Examples:

SP: *And Ioseph mette metels* A, VIII, 145;
Treuthe taugte me ones to louye hem B, VI, 211;
Caton a-cordeth ther-with C, X, 69.

PS: *Quath Perkyn the plougmon, "bi Peter ..."* A, VII, 3;
For, wot god, thei ... B, IV, 37;
Wot no man ... who is ... C, X, 69.

sP: *He halsed me* A, XII, 79;
I sey for me B, P, 201;
Ich sigge it for me C, I, 206.

Ps: *Sauh I neuere whimipeworthipyk* A, VII, 26;
For wit he neuere who is worthi B, VII, 78;
And seith hit the in herte C, II, 39.

Sp: *Bote mon is him lyk of marke* A, X, 32;
Leute shal don hym lawe B, III, 292;
Batailles shulle neuere eft be C, IV, 479.

pS: *Nis no mon him neih* A, XI, 47;
Shal neither kynge ne knygte ... ouer-lede B, III, 313;
Was no boggere so bolde bote-yf he blynde were C, IX, 201.

sp: *Bote he beo heihliche i-huret* A, VII, 300;
I may nougte stonde B, V, 394;
That is nogt resonable ne rect C. IV, 369.

ps: *And arn none ... souereynes in heuene* A, XI, 283;
Yet haue I no kynde knowing B, I, 136;
Yut can ich nother solfye ne synge C, VIII, 31.

The above figures reveal one striking feature, namely the fact that pS occurs about five times more frequently than the other varieties of the predicate-subject pattern. In other words, the pattern where a word with a light semantic load is followed by a word with heavy semantic load is found to occur most frequently. The pattern could be transcribed as 01.

If PS, Ps, pS, ps etc. are put into the notations 11, 10, 01, 00 etc. respectively, we find that in addition to the subjects and predicates, other categories (such as modifiers, particles etc.) will fit into the notations. This shift allows to view the problem of subject-predicate relations as thrown against the background of a much larger body of words which also exhibit the contrastive relation of units having only a grammatical and both grammatical and lexical function. A count that takes into consideration this enlarged number of units within the new notations, gives a picture which is much more clear cut and one that will allow to draw some conclusions as to the nature of the phenomenon of word order patterning in the examined texts.

1.1.6   The figures obtained from an analysis in which 11, 10, 01 and 00 notations were employed, suggests an underlying tendency to patterns where elements of unequal semantic-load are matched. Especially strong seems to be the sequence in which an initial light element is followed by a heavy one. Thus, for example, out of 186 cases of SP in Text A only 61 remained in group 11, while the rest (91 and 34 cases) joined group 01 and 10 respectively, since the given nominal subjects were found in direct juxtaposition with the full verbs only in these 61 instances. The immediate surroundings, in which a subject is found most frequently, is neither a heavy predicate, nor a heavy modifier, but a light modifier (as an article, a possessive pronoun) or a conjunction. Another example, but one that shows the thing from the opposite angle, is taken from Text B. Here out of 26 cases of PS only 9 remained in group 11, since the heavy predicate is found in immediate juxtaposition not with its heavy subject, but with some other words (particles, conjunctions) which possess a light semantic load. The remaining 17 instances of PS were included into the 01 group.[7]

It would be premature to conclude from the above that the occurrence of either the subject-predicate or the predicate-subject order is conditioned by the underlying pattern of two elements of unequal semantic load in juxtaposition. The next sections, however, will provide material to prove a hypothesis thus expressed.

The following tables show how the employment of 01 notations modifies the distribution of the subject-predicate and predicate-subject patterns.

Table XV

Text A

	ABSOLUTE NUMBER				PERCENTAGE			
	11	10	01	00	11	10	01	00
SP	61	34	91	—	32.8	18.3	48.9	0
PS	1	—	2		33.3	0	66.7	0
sP	—	—	205	—	0	0	100	0
Ps	—	6	—	—	0	100	0	0
Sp	—	61	69	—	0	46.9	53.1	0
pS	—	—	13	—	0	0	100	0
sp	—	—	—	207	0	0	0	100
ps	—	—	—	6	0	0	0	100

[7]   This is done not without difficulties, as in many cases the predicate (or subject) is both preceded and followed by a light element. Since, however, previous analyses, where the 01 notations have not been employed, revealed a marked tendency to patterns of light words followed by heavy ones, on the basis of analogy all doubtful cases will be included into the 01, not the 10 group. Due attention will be paid to this imperfection before any definite conclusions are reached.

Table XVI

Text B

ABSOLUTE NUMBER				PERCENTAGE			
11	10	01	00	11	10	01	00
SP	79	203	192	—	16.4	43.3	40.3	0
Ps	9	—	17	—	34.4	0	65.6	0
sP	—	—	459	—	0	0	100	0
Ps	—	11	—	—	0	100	0	0
Sp	—	77	179	—	0	30.0	70.0	0
pS	—	—	56	—	0	0	100	0
sp	—	—	—	528	0	0	0	100
ps	—	—	—	29	0	0	0	100

Table XVII

Text C

ABSOLUTE NUMBER				PERCENTAGE			
11	10	01	00	11	10	01	00
SP	123	210	176	—	24.1	41.3	34.6	0
PS	6	3	4	—	46.1	23.1	30.8	0
sP	—	—	464	—	0	0	100	0
Ps	—	11	—	—	0	100	0	0
Sp	—	118	215	—	0	35.4	64.6	0
pS	—	—	42	—	0	0	100	0
sp	—	—	—	623	0	0	0	100
ps	—	—	—	38	0	0	0	100

Examples:
(Numbers in brackets indicate the group-shift after the employment
of 01 notations.)

SP (11→10): *Concience with a crois com to preche* A, V, 11;
Faitures for fere fer-of flowen into bernes B, VI, 186;
Conscience to the clergie . . . *saide* C, I, 151.

SP (11→01): *And Pers, for puire teone, pollede hit a-sonder* A, VIII, 100;
The kynge fro conseille com B, III, 100;
Oure lord treuthe hem graunted C, X, 59.

PS (11→10): *Lereth hit this lewed men* A, 1, 125;
Wot no man . . . *who is* . . . C, X, 70.

PS (11→01): *But git sauereth not me thi siggynge* A, IX, 102;
And risen with ribaudye tho Roberdes knaues B, P, 44.

It will be observed that the "shift" affects only two patterns, namely SP and PS. In the case of the former, more than three quarters of the total "passed over" to either the 01 or the 10 group; the latter pattern "lost" more than a half. This adds to the evidence in favour of the hypothesis (stated above) that there exists a tendency to patterns where elements of unequal semantic load are matched.

The fact that sp and ps patterns have not been re-grouped at all, was dictated by consistency of method. Although it would be possible to differentiate between sp and ps patterns which are directly juxtaposed and those which are separated (or preceded) by particles, conjunctions and the like, such distinctions (as for instance between an auxiliary verb and a conjunction) are outside our definition of "semantic load". For this reason sp and ps patterns are excluded from table XVIII which summarizes Tables XV to XVII.

The most general and striking effect of the "shift" is a mean decrease in the percentage of 11 from 37.3% to 9.2% and a mean increase in the percentage of 01 from 39.2% to 68.3%.

1.1.7 Sections 1.1.5 and 1.1.6 have demonstrated the existence of two overlapping patterns. The numerical data, as presented on the tables, point to a very marked tendency to word sequences in which elements of unequal semantic load are juxtaposed

Table XVIII

	BEFORE "SHIFT"			AFTER "SHIFT"		
	TEXT A	TEXT B	TEXT C	TEXT A	TEXT B	TEXT C
11	(SP, PS) 34.9% (189)	(SP, PS) 39.0% (500)	(SP, PS) 37.9% (522)	11.4% (62)	6.9% (89)	9.4% (129)
10	(Ps, Sp) 25.0% (136)	(Ps, Sp) 20.4% (267)	(Ps, Sp) 25.2% (344)	18.6% (101)	22.8% (291)	25.0% (342)
01	(sP, pS) 40.1% (218)	(sP, pS) 40.6% (515)	(sP, pS) 36.9% (500)	70.0% (380)	70.3% (903)	65.6% (901)

(88.6%, 93.1% and 90.6% in the respective texts). In the present section an attempt will be made to show that the two patterns coincide with each other in a very characteristic way. This, it is hoped, will throw some light on the mechanism of word order patterning in the examined texts.

By comparing the distribution of the different varieties of subject-predicate and predicate-subject patterns within the 11, 10 and 01 groups, a characteristic curve is obtained, which seems to indicate that the dependence of word order patterns on the underlying structure as designed by the 01 notations is very strong indeed. It appears that, irrespective of whether the arrangement is subject-predicate or predicate-subject, the relation of word order patterns to the underlying "rhythmic" structure remains comparatively stable in all three texts of *Piers Plowman*. Since, as has been shown in the preceding sections, 11 relations occur least often and 01 relations most frequently, with 10 in the medium position, it is not surprising to find that the semantically heavy subjects and predicates, as well as their light equivalents, tend to occupy a position within the more, not the less typical "rhythmic" structure. From the fact that the semantic load relations are close to identical in both the subject-predicate and the predicate-subject patterns it follows that the former are better established in the language the three texts represent than the word order patterns.[8]

The numerical data are presented in the table below.

Table XIX

TEXT	SUBJECT-PREDICATE			PREDICATE-SUBJECT		
	11	10	01	11	10	01
A	11.4% (61)	17.8% (95)	70.8% (378)	4.6% (1)	27.2% (6)	68.2% (15)
B	6.7% (79)	23.3% (280)	70.0% (830)	9.7% (9)	11.8% (11)	78.5% (73)
C	11.3% (123)	30.1% (328)	58.6% (640)	9.1% (6)	21.1% (14)	69.8% (46)

Examples:
11: *Sothnesse sauh hem wel* A, II, 162;
Pacience apposed hym fyrste B, XIII, 222;
Mede maketh hym be by-loued C, IV, 269.
10: *God is muche in the gorge of theose grete maystres* A, XI, 53;
Mercy is a maydene there B, V, 644;
Batailles shulle neuere eft be C, IV, 479.
01: *Alle fledden for fere* B, 11, 233;
Hyt by-cometh for a kyng that ... C, IV, 266.

The following is a graphic representation of the parallel relations of subject-predicate and predicate-subject patterns to the "rhythmic" structure found in the texts. (. . . . . . is used for Text A, - - - - - for Text B and - . - . - . - . - for Text C.)

1.1.8   In order to pursue the line further, it is now proposed to examine sequences which are preceded by a prepositional. It is expected that since prepositionals are themselves either light or heavy (or mixed), their weight and that of the following subject

---

[8] It is, however, not intended here to claim that the structure, as expressed by the 01 notations, is "responsible" for the various subject-predicate relations, although later in the paper data will be presented, which will point to a conclusion not much unlike that.

Table XX

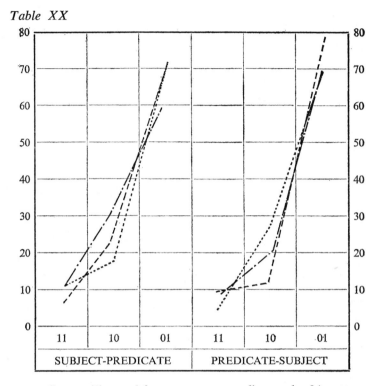

11	10	01	11	10	01
SUBJECT-PREDICATE			PREDICATE-SUBJECT		

or predicate will reveal features corresponding to the 01 patterns. One would be almost ready to state *a priori* that, knowing the semantic load of the prepositional, it is possible to predict the character of the following subject or predicate with some degree of statistical accuracy, if not the actual place of the subject and predicate in the sequence.

In the present section, wich aims at providing factual data for the first statement, attention will be concentrated chiefly on one word prepositionals, since phrases and clauses are of a complex "rhythmic" nature themselves, and as such of only restricted use for the present purpose. Excluded from the analysis are all sp and ps patterns, and that for the same reason as stated in section 1.1.6.

The examined prepositional sequences comprise 1444 cases

(Text A 272, Text B 513, Text C 659). Subject-predicate order is found in 953, predicate-subject order in 491 instances. The prepositionals have been grouped into four categories:

1. One word with light semantic load;
2. one word with heavy semantic load;
3. more words with light semantic load;
4. more words with at least one heavy member.

Only categories 1 and 2 are used for the purpose of argument, 3 and 4 will serve merely as auxiliary material. After the subject-predicate and predicate-subject patterns had been grouped according to the 01 notations, it was found that (with only slight deviations) the "rhythmic" and the word order patterns coincide in the expected way, that is, the majority of one word prepositionals with light semantic load preceded 11 and 10 patterns (SP, PS and Sp, Ps respectively), while most of the one word prepositionals with heavy semantic load were found before the 01 patterns (sP, pS).

The numerical data for the three texts are shown in the following table.

Table XXI

TEXT	CHARACTER OF PREPOSIT.	SUBJECT-PRED.			PRED.-SUBJECT		
		11	10	01	11	10	01
A	ONE WORD LIGHT	100% (20)	100% (1)	33.4% (14)	88.9% (8)	85,2% (23)	53.6% (22)
	ONE WORD HEAVY	0% (—)	0% (—)	66.6% (28)	11.1% (1)	14.8% (4)	46.4% (19)
B	ONE WORD LIGHT	100% (38)	100% (25)	39.2% (27)	100% (22)	83.2% (55)	32.3% (20)
	ONE WORD HEAVY	0% (—)	0% (—)	60.8% (42)	0% (—)	16.8% (11)	67.7% (42)
C	ONE WORD LICHT	100% (47)	100% (32)	43.1% (45)	100% (47)	100% (48)	54.6% (58)
	ONE WORD EAVY	0% (—)	0% (—)	56.9% (59)	0% (—)	0% (—)	45.4% (48)

The above table shows that prepositionals with light semantic load reach a percentage ranging from 100 to 83.2 when they precede 11 or 10 sequences. This agrees perfectly well with what was expected. According to expectations, light prepositionals should occur in front of 01 sequences in a percentage lower than 50. Although this is actually the case in Text B, the other two texts, while in agreement with the expected percentage in the subject-predicate sequences, show a reverse percentage in the predicate-subject group (53.6 : 46.4 and 54.6 : 45.6). In spite of this, however, the overall occurrence of light prepositionals before 01 sequences reaches only 44.0%.

Examples:

Subject-predicate, light prepositional:
11: *Thene Pers com to parlement* A, IV, 34;
  Thus "veniaunce, veniaunce" verrey charite asketh B, XVII, 289;
  Thenne Reson radde ryght a-non after C, XVI, 52.
10: *Thus Dowel and Dobet and Dobest the thridde beoth maystres* A, X, 14;
  Thanne contenence is nerre the croppe B, XVI, 69;
  So loue ys lech of lyue and lysse of alle peyne C, II, 200.
01: *"That thow wost wel", quod he* A, IX, 64;
  Thanne I frayned at Faith B, XVIII, 18;
  Thus go geueth goure golde C, I, 74.
Predicate-subject, light prepositional:
11: *Thenne mornede Mede* A, III, 163;
  Thanne gan Faith felly the fals Iuwes dispise B, XVIII, 92;
  Thenne cam Pilatus with muche peuple C, XXI, 35.
10: *Than maunged I with him* A, XII, 72;
  Thanne drowe I me amonges draperes B, V, 209;
  Thenne flammeth he as fuyr C, XX, 191.
01: *Ther was murthe and munstralsye Meede with to plese* A, III, 11;
  Thanne was Faith in a fenestre B, XVIII, 15;
  Thanne is Virginite more vertuous . . . as in heuene C, XIX, 89.
Subject-predicate, heavy prepositional:
01: *"Cesar" thei seiden* A, I, 49;
  And knelyng to the kyng clergeally he seyde B, P, 124;
  Wyghtliche he wente C, III, 217.

Predicate-subject, heavy prepositional:
11: *Grace hette the gate-ward* A, VI, 85;
     "Seteth" seith the kynge B, IV, 1.
10: *Luyte loueth he that lord that* ... A, XI, 49;
     "Contra" quod I as a clerke B, VIII, 20;
01: *Dredelen is Dobet* A, XI, 191;
     Witty is Treuthe B, II, 137;
     Dulle aren thy wittes C, II, 141.

The distribution of heavy prepositionals in relation to 11, 10 and 01 sequences also provides material that can serve to support the hypothesis. It is remarkable that the texts do not provide a single case of a heavy prepositional before 11 or 10 sequences in the subject-predicate patterns. In predicate-subject patterns, where they do occur before these sequences, the percentage is very low, 11.1, 14.8 and 16.8).

Inferences from distributional data as regards prepositionals belonging to categories 3 and 4 are of smaller value for the present purpose, especially in cases where the "rhythmic" structure of the given prepositional is very complex (clauses). However, when the two kinds of prepositionals are treated each as a whole in itself and their distribution analysed, the results are fairly close to those obtained with one word prepositionals. Thus prepositionals of category 3 are found most often before 11 and 10 sequences, those of category 4 usually occupy a position before 01 sequences. It seems, then, that prepositionals like "so then" (category 3) are analogous to prepositionals like "so" (category 1) as far as the differences in semantic load are concerned, while instances like "wilfuly" (category 2) correspond to such phrases as "with his ful wil" (category 4).

The distribution of light and heavy more-word prepositionals in 11, 10 and 01 sequences is presented on table XXII.

A comparison of the percentages as presented above with those shown in table XXI suggests that two (or more) light elements in the function of a prepositional possess a greater weight than one word light prepositionals, since the former do not occur before 11 sequences at all and their distribution before 10 is very

Table XXII

TEXT	CHARACTER OF PREPOSIT.	SUBJECT-PRED.			PRED.-SUBJECT		
		11	10	01	11	10	01
A	MORE WDS. LIGHT	—	—	9.7% (10)	—	11.1% (2)	36.8% (7)
	MORE WDS. HEAVY	—	—	90.3% (103)	—	88.9% (16)	63.2% (12)
B	MORE WDS. LIGHT	—	—	1.7% (3)	—	8.8% (3)	15.0% (3)
	MORE WDS. LIGHT	—	—	98.3% (205)	—	91.2% (31)	75.0% (17)
C	MORE WDS. LIGHT	—	—	6.6% (16)	—	0% (—)	35.0% (7)
	MORE WDS. HEAVY	—	—	93.7% (238)	—	100% (42)	65.0% (13)

limited (no occurrences in subject-predicate patterns, in predicate-subject patterns a lower percentage than in analogous sequences with one word light prepositionals). This is in agreement with what could be expected and seems to strengthen the validity of the hypothesis maintaining that there exists a close relationship between the semantic load of the prepositional and the semantic load of the subject or predicate that follows it. Perhaps it is even possible to modify the hypothesis by saying that the lighter the prepositional (one word light prepositionals are lighter than light prepositionals consisting of two or more words), the stronger the tendency to 11 and/or 10 patterns in subject and predicate relations.

In the case of heavy prepositionals consisting of more than one word the picture is not so clear. If heavy prepositionals consisting of more words were heavier than one-word heavy prepositionals, the occurrence of the former would have been much lower than is actually the case in 10 sequences (predicate-subject patterns); indeed, the occurrence would have been close to zero. However, it has to be born in mind that in very many instances the total number of light words in prepositionals of this category is greater than that of heavy words, and that the technique applied in the present work does not supply any safe criterion for evaluating the possible shades of differences in weight in these complex structures; neither is such evaluation vital for the sake of argument here. Still it is worth noticing that, except only 10 predicate-subject patterns, the obtained figures match our expectations.

1.1.9   In the present section the second hypothesis expressed at the beginning of section 1.1.8 will be tested: firstly, if (and to what extend) it is possible to predict the semantic load of a subject or predicate following a known prepositional; secondly, if (and to what extent) it is possible to predict the place of the subject and predicate in the sequence, once the semantic load of the prepositional is known.[9]

It was found that in the majority of cases light prepositionals were followed by subjects or predicates with heavy semantic load, while heavy prepositionals were usually followed by subjects or predicates having light semantic load. For light prepositionals the degree of predictability was highest in Text B (70.0% and 79.5%), for heavy prepositionals in Text C (100% and 98.0%). In general the degree of predictability is higher in cases of heavy prepositionals, the proportion being 92.7% to 65.6%.

Tables XXIII and XXIV present the data in detail.

A comparison of subject-predicate and predicate-subject sequences preceded by light and heavy prepositionals provided data for the following.

In all three texts light prepositionals are more often followed by predicate-subject then by subject-predicate order, while the reverse is true for heavy prepositionals. The highest degree of predictability in the case of light prepositionals is reached in Text A (60.2%), in the case of heavy prepositional in Text B

---

[9]   In order to achieve unambiguous results, only sequences with one word prepositionals were testes (cf. the objections to the value of multi-word prepositionals as stated in section 1.1.8).

Table XXIII

LIGHT PREPOSITIONAL

	TEXT A		TEXT B		TEXT C	
	SP	PS	SP	PS	SP	PS
EXPECTED (11, 10)	60.0% (21)	58.5% (31)	70.0% (63)	79.5% (77)	63.6% (79)	62.1% (95)
UNEXPECTED (01)	40.0% (14)	41.5% (22)	30.0% (27)	20.5% (20)	36.4% (45)	37.9% (58)

Table XXIV

HEAVY PREPOSITIONAL

	TEXT A		TEXT B		TEXT C	
	SP	PS	SP	PS	SP	PS
EXPECTED (01)	100% (28)	79.1% (19)	100% (88)	79.2% (42)	100% (99)	98.0% (48)
UNEXPECTED (11, 10)	0% (—)	20.9% (5)	0% (—)	20.8% (11)	0% (—)	2.0% (1)

(62.4%). The average predictability, however, is very low, namely 55.7% for light prepositionals and 59.4% for heavy ones. This difference, it will be noted, corresponds to the one established for the predictability of semantic load patterns.

The detailed results of the test are presented in the following table.

Table XXV

	TEXT A		TEXT B		TEXT C	
	SP	PS	SP	PS	SP	PS
LIGHT PREPOSITIONAL	39.8% (35)	60.2% (53)	48.3% (90)	51.7% (97)	44.8% (124)	55.2% (153)
HEAVY PREPOSITIONAL	54.0% (28)	46.0% (24)	62.4% (88)	37.6% (53)	61.9% (99)	38.1% (49)

1.2 *MIDDLE ENGLISH SERMONS*

1.2.1   In order to find where and to what extent the compared texts show similarities and differences, the process of analysis here will be proceeding along the same lines as in chapter 1.1.

Middle English Sermons contain 5540 instances of expressed subject and predicate which have been qualified as suitable for the purpose of the present study. Sentences, where the syntactic structure is not consistent (e.g. *Ryght so euery man that is here goinge in this werlde . . . lat hym do good werkes contynulye* 75, 32,[10] are not taken into consideration here. Macaronic constructions, if they affect either the subject or the predicate (as in *Euery synne that is donne in this werlde, aut est superbia vite aut concupicencia occulorum* 207, 9), are also excluded from the analysis.

In the available 5540 sentences, subject-predicate sequences are found in 4930 cases, predicate-subject sequences in 610, which constitutes 89 and 11 per cent of the total. The distribution of the respective orders in the text is fairly even, that is, in any random portion of the text, the number of instances of subject-predicate patterns will be about ten times larger than the number of predicate-subject patterns.

Examples:
> *Subject-predicate order:*
>> *Criste seid to ys disciples that . . .* 36, 5;
>> *"Lord, I am not worthy that thou goy . . .* 115, 27;
>> *And anone as thei sawe hym, thei toke hym* 64,9;.
> *Predicate-subject order:*
>> *Therfore seyth the holy apostell Seynt Poule . . . "Ambulate . . ."* 82, 19;
>> *I com not, seys Crist, for to call ryghtwis . . .* 164, 30;
>> *And git ther is many wicked lyvers that . . .* 134, 29.

1.2.2   After the analysed sentences had been grouped according to the presence or absence of a prepositional, the distribution of subject-predicate and predicate-subject patterns within these

---

[10]   The first number refers to the page, the second to the line.

groups was found to be very unequal. Only 6.5% of all the predicate-subject orders were found to occur in the non-prepositional group, which itself is larger than the prepositional group, the proportion between the two being 56.4% to 43.6%. It is assumed that such a discrepancy can hardly be accidental and the relation of the prepositional to the respective word order patterns will be studied in detail.

The contingency table below shows how the distribution of subject-predicate and predicate-subject patterns varies according to the presence or absence of a propositional.

Table XXVI

NO PREPOSITIONAL	PREPOSITIONAL
SP 3078 (2770)	1852 (2130) 4930
PS 40 (343)	570 (267) 610
3118	2422 5540

Since the discrepancy between the received numbers and those that would occur if word order patterns were in no sense connected with the presence or absence of prepositionals is large, the following formula is applied in order to receive the exact measure of association between the two variables.[11]

$$C = \sqrt{\frac{x^2}{N + x^2}}$$

$$x^2 = \sum_{i-1}^{r} \sum_{j-1}^{k} \frac{(Oij - Eij)^2}{Eij}$$

$$N = 5540 \qquad C = 0.33$$

[11]

$$x^2 = \frac{(3078 - 2770)^2}{2770} + \frac{(1852 - 2130)^2}{2130} + \frac{(40 - 343)^2}{343} + \frac{(570 - 267)^2}{267} = 682.5$$

$$C = \sqrt{\frac{682.5^2}{5540 + 682.5^2}} = 0.331$$

The distribution of subject-predicate and predicate-subject patterns in the prepositional and non-prepositional groups is represented graphically on the table below.

Examples:

 Subject-predicate, no prepositional:
  Who-so desireth worshipp . . . he shall fynde confucion
  208, 21;
  Ys Faders name was called Faustinianus 5, 23.
 Predicate-subject, no prepositional:
  And ther-fore seyth the grett clerke Hillarius 212, 3;
  And there-fore seys Seynt Iohn thus inys pistell 115, 4.
 Subject-predicate, with prepositional:
  Than this man was so wrouthe that . . . 169, 14;
  So be this procese thou seyst well that . . . 166,34.

*Table **XXVII***

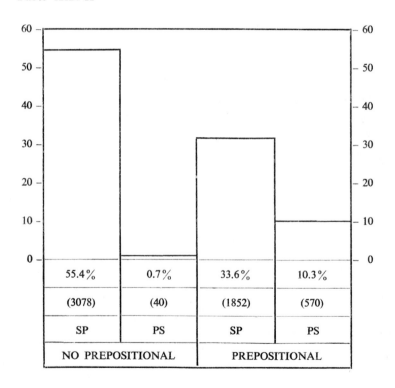

	55.4%	0.7%	33.6%	10.3%
	(3078)	(40)	(1852)	(570)
	SP	PS	SP	PS
	NO PREPOSITIONAL		PREPOSITIONAL	

Predicate-subject, with prepositional:
   Ryght so fareth it by mans liffe that . . . 75,6.
   For whan that we knalage oure trespase mekely, then
   maketh God vs for to speke . . . 148, 4.

1.2.3 The preceding section established the existence of a correlation between the occurrence of subject-predicate or predicate-subject patterns and the presence or absence of a prepositional in a given sequence. In the present section one aspect of the character of this correlation will be studied.

After all the prepositionals had been grouped according to their function in the sentence, the distribution of the two word order patterns was found to differ considerably in the various

Table XXVIII

	CHARACTER OF PREPOSITIONAL	PERCENTAGE OF PS	NUMBER OF PS
1.	Predicative	63.0%	29
2.	Object	42.0%	152
3.	Adverb of place	39.1%	97
4.	Adverb of manner	20.3%	106
5.	Adverb of time	17.2%	135
6.	Other	14.3%	58

groups. The number of predicate-subject patterns decreased gradually with the gradual decrease in closeness of relationship of the prepositional to the predicate. In other words, the closer was the connection of the prepositional with the predicate, the stronger the tendency to predicate-subject patterns.

The numerical data are presented in Table XXVIII.

The correlation between the two variables: frequency of predicate-subject occurrences and the character of the prepositional is shown graphically on the following table.

Table XXIX

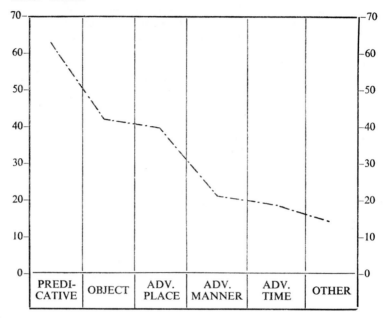

| PREDI-CATIVE | OBJECT | ADV. PLACE | ADV. MANNER | ADV. TIME | OTHER |

Examples:
> The prepositional is a predicative:
>> PS: *And ther-for cursed is the child* 119, 37;
>>   *Blynde was Adam when . . .* 146 ,18.
>> SP: *Dombe we ben of all goodness* 147, 15;
>>   *Defe he was when that he harde hym* 146, 21.
> The prepositional is an object:
>> PS: *"Ge, trewly" seid the Cristen clerke* 63, 29;
>>   *Figure and ensampull of this goynge finde we in holy-writte* 76, 1.
>> SP: *What is bodely lecherye ge knowen well i-nought* 24,15;
>>   *These thre faders thou muste wurshippe* 23,35.
> The prepositional is an abverb of place:
>> PS: *Also ther been moders the wiche that . . .* 119,19;
>>   *Here was than in hym grett holines* 4, 19.
>> SP: *And vn-to hym he shall com* 167, 4;
>>   *And in the shadowe of is fote he slepeth* 77, 12.
> The prepositional is an adverb of manner:
>> PS: *For thus seis oure Saueure . . .* 164, 29;

And so seyth Seynt Poule ... 210, 16.
SP: *Thus thou taketh vengeance* 37, 13;
And with-owte hym thou may do no good dede 119, 23
The prepositional is an adverb of time:
  PS: *Than seid the ermyte, "Sethen ..."* 38, 7;
  And than shall we fynde sekere and comforth 114, 29.
  SP: *Than in the tyme of kynges thei were delyvered* 1, 23;
  And as the gates were shett, oure Lord com and stode amyddes hem 134,10.
The prepositional is represented by other word(s):
  PS: *Ageyns suche speketh Crist in the gospell* 166, 27;
  And to suche on will I gladly be wedded to 80, 25.
  SP: *And gitt and thou wilte be perfite in the feygth, thou must do good werkes* 134, 34;
  Gytt for Cristes sake and for oure feygthe he toke cruwell passion 2, 38.

1.2.4 Predicate-subject order in non-prepositional sequences not only occurs rarely (6.5% as compared with PS occurrences in prepositional sequences), but is limited to one type of predicate and subject, namely to the noun and the full verb. The 40 cases of PS pattern also have another feature in common: the predicate is invariably preceded by a conjunction, that is, a word with light semantic load. In 13 instances the predicate is followed immediately by the subject, while in 27 cases a word having light semantic load stands between the subject and predicate. Thus all the predicate-subject orders in non-prepositional sequences form only two semantic load patterns: 011 and 0101.

Table XXX

PS	NUMBER OF INST.	PERCENTAGE
011	13	32.3
0101	27	67.7

Examples:
  011: *And ther-fore seith Dauid.* ... *"Et in lege ..."* 13, 36;
  And ther-fore seith Crist, "Ypocrite ..." 140, 12.

0101: *And ther-fore seiht the wise man Salomon . . .* 76, 32;
        And ther-fore seith the prophete, "Hec . . ." 118, 24.

It is remarkable that not a single instance of pure 11 configuration occurs in the predicate-subject non-prepositional group.

1.2.5 In the non-prepositional subject-predicate group the semantic load patterns, including the subjects and predicates themselves as well as their immediate neighbours, are distributed in the following way: In the SP patterns a heavy subject was found in immediate juxtaposition with a heavy predicate only in 127 instances, which constitutes 25%. In the rest of the cases a light element either preceded (64%) or followed the subject (11%). The semantic load patterns in the sP group show only the 01 pattern, since a pronominal subject is never found in immediate neighbourhood with a heavy word except the predicate itself. In 187 instances the nominal subject of the Sp pattern was preceded by a light modifier or a conjunction (23%), which resulted in a 010 pattern. The rest (73%) shows pattern 10. The pronominal subject in sp patterns is never preceded or followed by a heavy word, hence the semantic load pattern in these cases is always 00, and as such, excluded from the present count.

The overall distribution of semantic load patterns in the non-prepositional subject-predicate group presents the following picture:

Table XXXI

SP	NUMBER OF INST.	PERCENTAGE
11	127	6.1
10	681	32.9
01	1262	61.0

Examples:
   11: *Man lyveth not only in brade* 166, 8;
       Criste com to a seke man there he loye 213, 36.

   10: *Ihesus ys my loue* 78, 38;
       God will not here the preyour of . . . 213, 10.

01: *It happens often that he* . . . 140, 15;
Som sufred to be drawon on-lyve 2, 24.

1.2.6 After having found that 01 patterns constitute the majority of non-preprositional subject-predicate sequences, the second in frequency being the 10 pattern, and after having established that non-preprositional predicate-subject sequences ultimately show 01 patterns only, the present section will be devoted to the study of "rhythmic" relations of the prepositional to the subject or predicate following it. By analogy to the facts established for *Piers Plowman,* it is expected to find that there exists a correlation between the semantic load of the prepositional and the subject or predicate. As in the previous chapter, attention will be concentrated chiefly on one word prepositionals, which is even more justifiable in the *Sermons,* as "pure" heavy prepositionals occur comparatively rarely in the text presently analysed. Very frequently a multi-word prepositional is "summarized" by another prepositional which is added (almost always a light word), as for example in *But when that thei are riche, anon thei forgete God* 211,17, or *And giff we do so, than we shall haue grace* 45,28.

Out of the 2422 instances of prepositional sequences only 1696 have been qualified as of value for the purpose of the present analysis (726 cases with a pronominal subject and a light verb in the function of the predicate were excluded for the same reason as stated in section 1.1.6). Both light and heavy one-word prepositionals were found to occur with expected frequency only before 11 and 10 configurations; with 01 patterns the preportion of light to heavy prepositionals turned out to be the reverse of what was expected. Even when "mixed" prepositionals were treated as "pure" multi-word heavy ones, the expected balance was not reached. A closer examination of multi-word prepositionals did not give any hints as to the way of solving the difficulty, since expected results were obtained with patterns 01, but not with 10 or 11.

The numerical data are presented in the table below.

Table XXXII

CHARACTER OF PREPOSIT.	SUBJECT-PREDICATE			PREDICATE-SUBJECT		
	11	10	01	11	10	01
ONE WORD LIGHT	96.1% (52)	88.0% (88)	53.7% (102)	95.5% (84)	56.5% (13)	54.7% (106)
ONE WORD HEAVY	3.9% (5)	12.0% (12)	46.3% (88)	4.5% (4)	43.5% (10)	45.3% (34)
MORE WDS. LIGHT	18.9% (14)	6.5% (10)	17.3% (45)	11.8% (9)	3.3% (2)	2.4% (4)
MORE WDS. HEAVY	81.1% (68)	93.5% (146)	82.7% (471)	88.2% (75)	96.7% (58)	97.6% (75)

For the sake of consistency with the procedure adopted in the analysis of *Piers Plowman,* data from the group of multi-word prepositionals will not be used to counterbalance the situation as found in the group which, for other reasons, is regarded as best suited for the purpose of the study. The argument, then, that where one-word prepositionals do not show the expected percentage, multi-word prepositionals do, and conversely, will not be forwarded here. Instead, it is pointed out that within the group of one word prepositionals the discrepancies between the numbers are considerable (96.1 : 3.9; 88.0 : 12.0; 95.5 : 4.5; 56.5 : 43.5) when the larger numbers speak in favour of the general argument of the thesis, but slight (53.7 : 46.3; 54.7 : 45.3) when the larger numbers speak against it. The overall proportion, then, can be considered as in agreement with the statement that there exists a correlation between the semantic load of the prepositional and that of the subject or predicate, whichever of the two happens to follow it.

Examples:
   Subject-predicate, light prepositional:
      11: *Then God made man and gave hym* ... 102, 5;
           And so Seynt Iohn Crisostome wittenesse and seith 23,
      13.

10: *And than God will quyte youre mede* 8, 30;
And thus grete swerers may drede full sore 117, 30.

01: *Ther he seis thus, "Abiciamus . . ."* 167, 36;
And that I preye euery man and womman conne and beleue 14, 13.

Predicate-subject, light prepositional:

11: *Than seid Crist vn-to hym* 134, 18;
Than maketh God vs for to speke 148, 4.

10: *And so lese I my loue* 81, 12;
Than seid thei, "Tell vs . . ." 64, 15.

01: *Here arn resceyved synners* 162, 25;
Also ther been moders the whiche that . . . 119, 19.

Subject-predicate, heavy prepositional:

11: *But suerly evell leuers peruerteth thise tymes* 273, 15;
And questionlesse God loueth hem moste 107, 23.

10: *Certenly synne is the cause* 212, 33;
And trewly this doying is wondirfull 263, 25.

01: *Sonne, wele thou wote that what I haue . . .* 169, 27;
"Sustur" he said, "latt this . . ." 148, 25.

Predicate-subject, heavy prepositional:

11: *"Trewly" seid the Cristen clerke* 63, 35;
Of suche men speketh Dauid in the . . . 75, 19.

10. *And nogthe spake he but as was in ys herte* 78, 35;
"For-sothe" seith he, "wickednes . . ." 207, 6.

01: *But now-adaies old men ben full of vices* 119, 36;
Blynde was Adam whan that he sawe the eddur 146, 19.

1.2.7 The preceding section provided data showing that there exists a correlation between the semantic load of the prepositional and the semantic load pattern that follows it. It was also established that certain configurations of semantic load are equally valid for the subject-predicate as for the predicate-subject order. It is now possible to test the predictability of semantic load patterns following a known prepositional, as well as the word order pattern following a known prepositional. It will be remembered that the difficulties mentioned in the preceding section had their source in the fact that the absolute number of light prepositionals was higher than that of heavy prepositionals. In the present test in each procedure only one type or prepositional is involved.

The hypothesis is that a light prepositional tends to be followed by a "rhythmic" structure beginning with a heavy element, while a heavy prepositional is usually found before a pattern which starts with a light element. The numerical data are found in the following table.

Table XXXIII

		SUBJECT-PREDICATE	PREDICATE-SUBJECT
LIGHT PREPOSIT.	EXPECTED (11.10)	58.0% (140)	70.4% (97)
	UNEXPECTED (01)	42.0% (102)	29.6% (41)
HEAVY PREPOSIT.	EXPECTED (01)	83.8% (88)	70.8% (34)
	UNEXPECTED (11,10)	16.2% (17)	29.2% (14)

As can be seen, the predictability of semantic load patterns is fairly high, except for the light prepositionals in subject-predicate sequences.

The results of the test for predictability of subject-predicate *vs.* predicate-subject patterns are presented in the following table.

Table XXXIV

	SUBJECT-PREDICATE	PREDICATE-SUBJECT
LIGHT PREPOSIT.	63.6% (242)	36.4% (138)
HEAVY PREPOSIT.	68.6% (105)	31.4% (48)

Although the test is not negative as such, it has little value in the context of the examined material, since it had been found previously that subject-predicate sequences occur most frequently in non-prepositional sentences. The test would be positive for our purposes, if the table indicated a much higher discrepancy between the cell values. This, however, cannot be expected if, as has been stated above, the semantic load of prepositionals matches the semantic load patterns of subject-predicate and predicate-subject orders indiscriminately.

1.3 SUMMARY

The relation of subject-predicate to predicate-subject order is 77.6% to 22.4% [12] in *Piers Plowman,* and 89.0% to 11.0% in *Middle English Sermons.* The distribution of the respective orders varies according to the presence or absence of prepositionals. Only a small percentage of predicate-subject patterns is found in non-prepositional clauses, the figures for the respective texts being 14.8 and 6.5.

A marked tendency to a juxtaposition of elements of unequal semantic load (01, 10) was observed. Word order patterns and semantic load patterns revealed close similarities in distribution: The frequency curve of semantic load patterns in the subject-predicate group has an almost identical shape as the analogous curve for predicate-subject sequences. The typical semantic load patterns are more abundantly represented in non-typical than in typical word order patterns.

Prepositionals were found to influence word order patterns a) directly and b) indirectly. The influence is direct when the percentage of predicate-subject occurrences depends on the syntactic relationship between the prepositional and the predicate (cf. Tables XX and XXIX), indirect, when the semantic load of the prepositional influences the semantic load pattern of what follows, that is, very often the semantic load pattern of subject and predicate, and consequently their order.

In all the features under discussion the differences between the given texts are slight, the highest discrepancy reaching only 11.4%.

[12] All the percentages given in the summary are the averages of the three texts.

2. THE RELATION OF THE PREDICATE TO OTHER ELEMENTS IN THE CLAUSE

2.1 *PIERS PLOWMAN*

2.1.1   The larger the number of words in the clause, the larger – theoretically at least – the number of positions which the predicate can occupy. Three main positions can be distinguished: initial, medial, final.

Initial position can occur only in predicate-subject patterns, and since in these patterns the predicate is invariably followed either by the subject or a light subject modifier followed by the subject, this configuration has been exhaustively analysed in the preceding chapter. The same refers to to all medial positions of the predicate-subject pattern. Consequently all predicate-subject patterns are excluded from the present chapter. Also excluded are all subject-predicate sequences in clauses consisting of two elements only, as there exists only one possible position for the predicate.

For the purpose of the present study it is proposed to distinguish between the following positions the predicate assumes:

I.   The predicate follows the subject immediately, but is followed by any number of other words;

II.   the predicate is separated from its subject by at least one word and followed by at least one word; (medial position);[1]

III.   the predicate is separated from its subject by at least one word and is followed by space (final position).

2.1.2   After the elimination of doubtful cases (e.g. *Bote Salamon the sage a sarmoun he made* A, III, 84), the number of clauses suitable for the present analysis amounted to 1333 in Text A, 3277 in Text B, and 3447 in Text C. In most instances

---

[1]   This is not an unambiguous definition. It should be added that it includes a number of clauses where the subject is not expressed.

the predicate was found to follow its subject immediately (average percentage: 52.3). The second largest group formed clauses with their predicates in the final position (average percentage 29.3), while it was found to occur least frequently in medial position. The following table presents the distribution in detail.

Table XXXV

	TEXT A	TEXT B	TEXT C
I	47.4% (632)	54.2% (1777)	55.4% (1911)
II	22.5% (300)	15.6% (509)	16.3% (561)
III	30.1% (401)	30.2% (991)	28.3% (975)

When a distinction between main and subordinate clauses was made, the distribution was found to be different in the two groups. The average percentage for the medial position was practically identical in both groups (18.2% and 18.1%), but predicates were found in the final position more frequently in subordinate than in main clauses (average percentages: 23.8 and 36.5), while the reverse was true for predicates occupying the first position after the subject (average percentage: 45.1 and 58.0).

Table XXXVI

		TEXT A	TEXT B	TEXT C
Main clauses	I	50.0% (360)	60.9% (1049)	63.2% (1234)
	II	26.0% (187)	15.8% (272)	12.8% (251)
	III	24.0% (173)	23.3% (401)	24.0% (467)
Subordinate clauses	I	44.3% (272)	46.8% (728)	45.2% (677)
	II	18.4% (113)	15.2% (237)	20.7% (310)
	III	37.3% (228)	38.0% (590)	34.1% (508)

The fluctuations within the three texts, as seen on the above table, are slight. Differences between the cell values on the horizontal line range, in most cases, between 0.1% and 5.0%. Only Text A shows greater differences (up to 10.9%) in four cells. The figures for subordinate clauses are remarkably similar in all three texts.

Since predicates were found to occur in a given position with different frequencies in main and subordinate clauses, the two groups will be kept apart in the present analysis.

Examples:
  Main clauses:
    I: *I schop me in-to a schroud* A, P, 2;
       Thus the poete preues that . . . B, XII, 260;
       And so they leueden bothe C, XVIII, 20.
    II: *Corteisliche the kyng thenne com to Resoun* A, IV, 31;
       Ac Pacience in the paleis stode B, XIII, 29;
       Many sondry sorwes in cytees fallen ofte C, IV, 90.
    III: *This leornden this leches and lettres him senden* A, II, 199;
       I can no pardon fynde B, VII, 112;
       And loue hue me broughte C, XII, 169.

  Subordinate clauses:
    I: *Whon he drouh to the dore, then . . .* A, V, 200;
       Gif that I lye, Mathew . . . B, VII, 60;
       . . . that ich lacke richesse, thauh . . . C, XIV, 26.
    II: *. . . that he ne worth siker saaf* A, VIII, 55;
       . . . and how . . . no corps in her kirkegerde ne in her kyrke was buryed B, XIII, 9;
       . . . and blew . . . that alle seyntes with synful men songen with Dauid C, VIII, 154.
    III: *. . . that out of lawe libbeth* B, X, 25;
       . . . that shame me thougte A, XII, 16;
       . . . that oute briddes and bestes by here makes geden C, XIV, 136.

2.1.3   In the chapter devoted to subject-predicate relations it was established that word order is found in conformity with the typical semantic load patterns. The following sections aim at finding if, and to what extent, the position which the predicate assumes in relation to the other elements in the sequence also depends on these patterns.

In the first stage of the analysis all main clauses have been grouped according to the semantic load of the predicate and that of the word immediately preceding it. Thus in the notations 11, 10, 01, and 00 the latter symbol stands for the predicate.

By analogy to the results obtained in the previous chapter, it is expected that pattern 01 will include more instances than any other pattern, or even more than all the other patterns together. This is actually the case in all three positions of the predicate, the mean percentages for the three texts being: 56.4 in position I, 49.2 in position II, and 63.8 in position III. The received values, however, did not meet with what was expected in the case of patterns 11 and 10. According to our hypothesis the typical, that is the most frequent pattern, is the one in which words of unequal semantic load are matched. The mean percentages, however, namely 16.9 (I), 37.1 (II), 34.2 (III) for pattern 11, and 11.0 (I), 7.7 (II), 0 (III) for pattern 10, seem to suggest that the hypothesis, although true for subject-predicate relations, cannot be maintained in the case of the relation of the predicate to the other elements in the sequence. Especially strong evidence against the hypothesis seems to be the fact that 10 patterns do not occur at all in any of the three texts in a final position. The high percentage of 11 patterns, which also speaks against the hypthesis, will be accounted for in section 2.1.4.

The distribution of the predicate (second symbol in the 01 notations) in the three positions is shown on the next page.

2.1.4   In the preceding section only the element standing immediately before the predicate was taken into consideration. However, in position I and II the word following it also can be treated as forming "rhythmic" patterns with the predicate. In the second stage of the analysis, then, all main clauses will be grouped according to the semantic load of the predicate and that of the word immediately following it. Thus in the notations 11, 10, 01 and 00 the former symbol will stand for the predicate.

Table XXXVII

	TEXT A			TEXT B			TEXT C		
	I	II	III	I	II	III	I	II	III
11	17.0% (63)	30.5% (57)	26.0% (45)	13.3% (139)	34.9% (95)	46.4% (186)	19.3% (243)	45.8% (115)	30.1% (141)
10	12.7% (47)	9.1% (17)	0% (—)	9.0% (95)	7.7% (21)	0% (—)	11.4% (131)	6.3% (16)	0% (—)
01	53.5% (198)	53.5% (100)	74.0% (128)	59.5% (624)	57.4% (156)	52.4% (210)	56.3% (706)	36.8% (92)	64.8% (303)
00	16.8% (62)	6.9% (13)	0% (—)	18.2% (191)	0% (—)	1.2% (5)	14.0% (174)	11.1% (28)	5.0% (23)

The numerical data are very revealing indeed. 11 patterns were found only in 7.4% in position I and in 6.3% in position II. The fact that the number of 01 patterns is very small is not disturbing at all; on the contrary, this is expected, especially in view of the fact that 10 patterns, which were poorly represented when the predicate was matched with the neighbour in front of it, reach the mean percentage of 65.5 in position I and 80.3 in position II.

Full numerical data showing the predicate occurrences in positions I and II are presented on the following page, where the first symbol of the 01 notations stands for the predicate.

From the preceding and the present section it follows that the predicate, whether immediately preceded by its subject, or surrounded by other elements is most often found in juxtaposition with at least one element whose semantic load is different from that which it itself possesses. This agrees with the hypothesis, stated in the preceding chapter, that word order patterns tend to be formed within the typical semantic load patterns. It has also been demonstrated in the preceding chapter that there exists a very strong tendency to form subject-predicate patterns to the disfavour of the reverse order. The two tendencies (to the typical

Table XXXVIII

	TEXT A		TEXT B		TEXT C	
	I	II	I	III	I	II
11	4.6% (17)	7.5% (14)	7.8% (82)	6.3% (17)	10.0% (125)	3.4% (9)
10	66.0% (244)	76.5% (143)	64.9% (681)	86.0% (234)	65.7% (824)	79.0% (198)
01	20.5% (76)	9.1% (17)	19.6% (205)	7.7% (21)	12.4% (155)	6.4% (16)
00	8.9% (33)	6.9% (13)	7.7% (81)	0% (—)	11.9% (150)	11.2% (28)

semantic load pattern and the typical word order) are of different natures and may, at times, set in conflicting directions. This seems to account for the situation as seen on table XXXVIII. The number of the typical 10 occurrences is smaller when the predicate follows its subject immediately than when it assumes a position between other members of the sequence, the mean difference being as high as 14.8%. This is not surprising, because once the sequence offers a convenient configuration in which the semantic load of the predicate can form a typical "rhythmic" pattern with other words than the subject, the chances that the predicate will seek its place next to the subject are smaller than they would be otherwise. And conversely, the subject will attract its predicate even against the tendency to form typical semantic load patterns. More of it will be said in the following section.

2.1.5 It is now proposed to study the place of the predicate in the sequence and the relation of its semantic load not only to one of its neighbours, but to the words both preceding and following it. The semantic load patterns, then, will consist of three elements, the symbol in the middle standing for the predicate itself. Naturally, only space is not regarded as an element having a 0 semantic load.

The possible combinations of the three symbols are

$$111, 010, 110, 001$$
$$101, 000, 100, 011$$

and they all occur in the texts.

111 patterns have been found to occur very rarely, the mean percentage being 5.4 for position I and 2.4 for position II. The fact that in position I this non-typical pattern reaches the relative double number of the same configuration in position II, speaks in favour of the statement (section 2.1.4) that the subject is capable of attracting its predicate even against the tendency to form typical semantic load patterns. The 111 configuration in position II is non-typical in a double sense ("rhythmic" pattern and separation of the predicate from its subject), while the same configuration in position I is non-typical only in one way ("rhythmic" pattern). It is probably for this reason that the predicate is found to occur twice as often in position I as compared with position II.

The point will be seen even more clearly if it is stressed that in all configurations the absolute number of predicate occurrences in position II is much lower than that in position I. This being the case, the percentage calculated from the total is not fully representative of the problem in question. A comparison of positions I and II, based on figures from pattern 111 only, gives a picture in which the differences are considerably more pronounced.[2]

On the other hand the pattern, in which a heavy predicate is surrounded by two semantically light elements is most abundantly represented. The average percentages are 54.4 for position I and 45.8 for position II. This proportion is also in agreement

---

[2] The occurrence of 000 is also low (average percentage: 6.5 for position I and 6.0 for position II), but since this pattern, strictly speaking, does not represent three elements of equal semantic load, it can be left out of consideration.

Table XXXIX

POSITION	PATTERN 111		
	TEXT A	TEXT B	TEXT C
I	63.2% (12)	100% (62)	90.1% (90)
II	36.8% (7)	0% (—)	9.9% (9)

with the hypothesis as stated above. Since in this case the semantic load pattern and the tendency to an immediate juxtaposition of the subject and predicate are not in conflict, position I has a higher occurrence than position II. This is especially evident if, analogously to the case described above, figures from pattern 010 only are compared.

Table XL

POSITION	PATTERN 010		
	TEXT A	TEXT B	TEXT C
I	67.5% (193)	81.2% (604)	88.0% (671)
II	32.5% (93)	18.8% (139)	12.0% (92)

Analogous proportions are found in the reverse pattern, that is, when a light predicate is surrounded by two words with heavy semantic load (101). Again the percentage calculated from all the patterns in one and the other position does not give a clear picture, because of the smaller absolute number of predicate occurrences in position II as compared with position I. However, if pattern 101 is singled out and the proportion of predicates found in the two positions compared, it becomes clear that this pattern also provides evidence for the hypothesis, since predicates occur in position I more than three times as often as they do in position II.

Table XLI

POSITION	PATTERN 101		
	TEXT A	TEXT B	TEXT C
I	69.7% (39)	77.5% (72)	82.0% (73)
II	30.3% (17)	22.5% (21)	18.0% (16)

The graph on p. 61 summarizes the problem under discussion, showing the different levels and shapes of the curves, as well as the extent to which the three texts of *Piers Plowman* differ from one another. (. . . . . is used for Text A, - - - - - for Text B, - . - . -. - .- for Text C.)

The strongest evidence for the hypothesis is provided by pattern 100. A light predicate preceded by a heavy word and followed by a light one has not been found in the medial position in any of the texts. The suggested interpretation of this fact is that, since the heavy subject is a good match for the light predicate, there is no reason why the latter should seek its position away from the former.

While in configuration 100 the discrepancy between predicate occurrences in the respective positions has reached the utmost degree (100% to 0%), the opposite happens in pattern 110, where the mean discrepancy is very small indeed (51.3% to 48.7%). If our hypothesis is correct, no other proportion should be expected, since it is exactly in this pattern that a certain balance is achieved: Although the predicate cannot form a typical semantic load pattern with the subject, yet the presence of the other light element is a kind of compensation. On the other hand even in a medial position this pattern is somewhere between

Table XLII

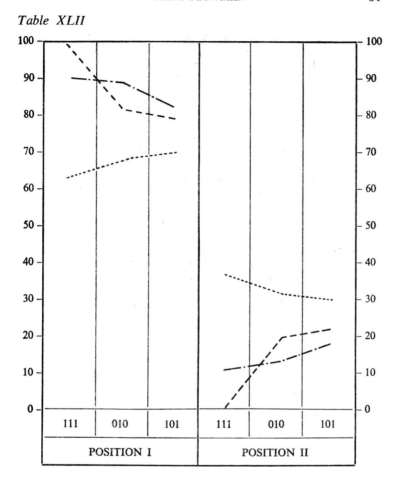

the two extremes, the very typical 010 and the very non-typical 111.

Examples:

> *Position I:*
>> 111: *"Crist wot", quod Clergie, "knowe hit gif the lyke* A, XII, 1;
>> *And Piers Plowman parceyued plenere tyme* B, XVI, 103;
>> *Her-of the olde made bokes* C, XII, 149;

010: *For-thi I lere gou* A, III, 61;
Thai conse nasore mynstralscye B, X, 43;
And alle thre bote on God C, XI, 155.

101: *For rihtfoliche resoun schulde rulen ou alle* A, I, 52;
And that conscience and Crist hath yknitte faste B,
XV, 237;
Bote men of holichurche sholde receyue ryght naught
C, XVIII, 42.

100: *And Clotoun was a gret cherl* A, V, 204;
Mathew is to blame B, VII, 60;
Here ioie hath no ende C, XIV, 26.

110: *For non likerous lyflode heore licam to plese* A, P, 30;
Thise foure the fader of heuene made to this folde
B, VII, 53;
Kynges and cardinales knowen hym som tyme C,
XVII, 365.

Position II:

111: *Heade of misdoors maketh men so riche* A, III, 278;
(no occurrences in Text B)
Ac the poure pacient purgatorie passeth C, XIV, 31.

010: *Corteisliche the kyng thenne com to Resoun* A, IV, 31;
Pers thenne pollede hit B, III, 116;
Holy churche here-of can the lere C, XII, 147;

101: *Preres . . . for knowynge of comers, kepten him* A,
II, 206;
The creatures . . . of kynde ben engendred B, XIII, 18;
Kynges . . . that . . . ruelen the comune, han pardon
C, X, II.

100: (no occurrences)

110: *A louely ladi . . . in linnene i-clothed, com a-doun* A,
I, 4;
The prophete his payn ete in penaunce B, VII, 121;
Thus thorgh Hende-speche entrede the frere C, XXIII,
354.

The fact that in the remaining patterns a regularity, which would be comparable to that of 111, 010, 101, 110 and 100, has not been discovered, may be due to our definition of semantic load, which makes no finer distinction than between heavy and light, and also to the relative scarcity of predicate occurrences in the remaining groups, which leaves room for accidental relations. For the sake of completeness, however, all the numerical data are included in the following table, which accounts for the overall distribution of the predicate in the two positions.

Table XLIII

	TABLE A		TABLE B		TABLE C	
	I	II	I	II	I	II
111	3.2% (12)	3.7% (7)	5.8% (62)	0% (—)	7.2% (90)	3.6% (9)
010	52.1% (193)	49.6% (93)	57.6% (604)	51.1% (139)	53.5% (671)	36.7% (92)
110	13.8% (51)	26.8% (50)	7.4% (77)	34.9% (95)	12.2% (153)	42.2% (106)
011	1.4% (5)	3.8% (7)	1.9% (20)	6.3% (17)	2.8% (35)	0% (—)
101	10.5% (39)	9.2% (17)	6.9% (72)	7.7% (21)	5.9% (73)	6.4% (16)
000	6.8% (25)	6.9% (13)	5.5% (58)	0% (—)	7.3% (92)	11.1% (28)
100	2.2% (8)	0% (—)	2.2% (23)	0% (—)	4.6% (58)	0% (—)
001	10.0% (37)	0% (—)	12.7% (133)	0% (—)	6.5% (82)	0% (—)

2.1.6   In subordinate clauses the distribution of the predicate in the three positions differs from that in main clauses. The discrepancies, however, affect chiefly position III.

In the analysis a parallel procedure to that used for the study of main clauses was adopted, that is, in the first stage all subordinate clauses have been grouped according to the semantic load of the predicate and that of the word immediately preceding it, so that in the notations 11, 10, 01 and 00, the latter symbol represented the predicate itself.

In subordinate clauses, similarly to the case of main clauses, the highest mean number of predicate occurrences is included in pattern 01. This, however, is true only for positions I and II, where the respective figures are 41.6% and 39.1%. In position III pattern 01 reaches only 28.6%, which is less than the percentage for the same position in pattern 11 (31.9). Positions I and II in pattern 11 are represented by 11.0% and 25.6% respectively.

It will be remembered that the analysis of main clauses revealed a fairly high proportion of predicate occurrences in the final position, in spite of the fact that the immediate neighbour of the heavy predicate is a heavy word too. In the subordinate clauses the proportions are even more pronounced.

Light predicates preceded by heavy words are very evenly distributed in all three positions and in all three texts, the relative number being fairly close to 25% all through. The reverse is true for pattern 00, which does not seem to reflect any regularity in distribution. This, however, is not surprising, for the 00 notation, strictly speaking, does not really represent two elements of equal semantic load.

The following table shows the distribution in detail.

Table XLIV

	TEXT A			TEXT B			TEXT C		
	I	II	III	I	II	III	I	II	III
11	9.5% (26)	21.2% (24)	32.9% (75)	12.2% (89)	30.3% (72)	39.5% (233)	13.8% (93)	25.2% (78)	41.4% (210)
10	23.2% (63)	21.2% (24)	18.0% (41)	23.1% (168)	26.6% (63)	24.4% (144)	15.5% (104)	26.8% (83)	36.0% (183)
01	41.2% (112)	54.0% (61)	38.6% (88)	37.0% (269)	28.3% (67)	34.6% (204)	47.6% (323)	28.7% (89)	12.6% (64)
00	26.1% (71)	3.6% (4)	10.5% (24)	27.7% (202)	14.8% (35)	1.5% (9)	23.1% (157)	19.3% (60)	10.0% (51)

If the cell values of the above table are compared with those of table XXXVII, it will be noticed that in main clauses position III in patterns 10 and 00 is either not represented at all, or is represented very poorly. In subordinate clauses these patterns occur more frequently, though even here the mean percentage is only 26.1 and 7.3 respectively. If patterns 11, 10, 01 and 00 are singled out so that the absolute numbers of predicate occurrences in position III can be compared, it is found that in main clauses almost all cases of the predicate in a final position are included in patterns 11 and 01 (in spite of the fact that 11 is an unfavourable semantic load pattern), in subordinate clauses the proportion is less striking, but here too patterns 00 and 10 constitute only one third of patterns 11 and 01. This being the case, the following can be stated:

Predicates having light semantic load avoid the final position in the clauses much more than do predicates with heavy semantic load. This tendency is realized to a higher degree in main than in subordinate clauses. The following table supports the above statement.

Table XLV

	PATT.	ABSOL. NR. IN TEXTS	%	ABSOL. NR. OF 11.01 & 10.00	% OF 11.01 & 10.00
MAIN CLAUSES:	11	372	35.7	1013	97.3
	01	641	61.6		
	10	—	0	28	2.7
	00	28	2.7		
SUBORD. CLAUSES:	11	418	37.7	774	69.8
	01	356	32.1		
	10	249	22.5	333	30.2
	00	84	7.7		

2.1.7   In the present section, which is devoted to the study of predicate positions in their relation to the element immediately following it, all occurrences of end position of the predicate are automatically excluded. Hence only positions I and II will be dealt with here, and in the notations 11, 10, 01 and 00 the first symbol represents the predicate.

As expected, the highest occurrence in both positions were found with patterns 10 and 01, while the two non-typical patterns (11 and 00) are poorly represented. The mean percentages for 10 and 01 are in position I 40.8 and 37.6, in position II 59.8 and 24.5 respectively, for 11 and 00 in position I 13.0 and 8.6, in position II 2.7 and 13.0 respectively. These proportions are in complete agreement with the main hypothesis of the present study. Moreover, as seen on the following table, in this respect the subordinate clauses are almost perfectly balanced, the only disturbing feature being the low percentage of 01 occurrences in position II in Text A.

Table XLVI

	TEXT A		TEXT B		TEXT C	
	I	II	I	II	I	II
11	8.4% (23)	6.2% (7)	11.8% (86)	1.6% (4)	18.8% (127)	0.3% (1)
10	42.3% (115)	69.0% (78)	37.4% (272)	57.0% (135)	42.7% (289)	53.5% (166)
01	41.2% (112)	9.8% (11)	43.3% (315)	31.6% (75)	28.3% (192)	32.0% (99)
00	8.1% (22)	15.0% (17)	7.6% (55)	9.8% (23)	10.2% (69)	14.2% (44)

2.1.8   In positions I and II the predicate can form semantic load patterns with its neighbouring elements. In the case of the former position the word preceding it is its subject, in the case of the latter none of the two neighbours is the subject. The relation of the predicate to both these words will be dealth with in the present section, and it will be attempted to establish to what extent the position of the predicate is influenced by the semantic load patterns which it can form with its immediate neighbours. As in section 2.1.5, the following patterns will be considered here:

111, 010, 110, 011,

101, 000, 100, 001,

where the predicate is represented by the symbol standing in the middle.

111 patterns have been found to be of comparatively rare occurrence, the mean percentage for position I being 2.4, for position II 1.3, that is, if the percentage is based on the calculation of all the predicate occurrences in the two positions, the heavy predicate, when surrounded by the two other heavy words, may be said to occur in position I nearly twice as often as in position II. However, the proportion is more striking if the percentage is based on the numbers within pattern 111 only. Such a count has shown that the predicate is found in position I in 86.0%, and only in 14.0% in position II. This result is comparable to that obtained for main clauses in the analogous situation (cf. Table XXXIX). The flucuations between the particular texts of *Piers Plowman* are seen on the table below.

Table XLVII

POSITION	PATTERN 111		
	TEXT A	TEXT B	TEXT C
I	71.5% (5)	72.8% (14)	96.0% (24)
II	28.5% (2)	27.2% (4)	4.0% (1)

The fact that also in subordinate clauses heavy predicates surrounded by heavy words are found in such a small proportion supports the statement about the non-typical character of 111

patterns. Predicates, which nevertheless do occur in these unfavourable surroundings, are found more often in position I than
in position II. This again strengthens the hypothesis about the
conflicting tendencies which account for the variety of word
order patterns.

The same is seen from the opposite angle if the most typical
pattern, namely 010, is considered. Here no conflicting tendencies exist, and it is expected that the proportion of predicates in
immediate juxtaposition with their subjects should be higher than,
for instance, in the case of pattern 111. This is actually the case,
the mean percentage for the three texts being 71.1 in position I
and 28.9 in position II. The following table shows the fluctuations
between the texts.

Table XLVIII

PATTERN 010			
POSITION	TEXT A	TEXT B	TEXT C
I	62.6% (94)	79.6% (197)	71.2% (220)
II	37.4% (56)	20.4% (67)	28.8% (89)

The proportion based on the total of predicate occurrences in
the two positions is not only less striking (as in the cases above),
but misleading, since it is position II that has the higher figure
(mean 35.5) and position I the lower (mean 31.5%).

In the reverse pattern, that is 101, similar proportions are
found. Although the percentages calculated from the total do
reflect the problem to some extent (mean 18.0% in position I
and 13.5% in position II), the figures based on a count of
occurrences within the 101 pattern only are more revealing (mean
77.0% and 23.0% in the respective positions). The table below
shows the absolute numbers as well as the differences between
the texts.

Table XLIX

PATTERN 101			
POSITION	TEXT A	TEXT B	TEXT C
I	88.4% (53)	79.0% (151)	63.5% (94)
II	11.6% (7)	21.0% (40)	36.5% (54)

The following graph summarizes Tables XLVII to XLIX (. . . . .
is used for Text A, - - - - - for Text B, - . - . -. -. - for Text C).

Table L

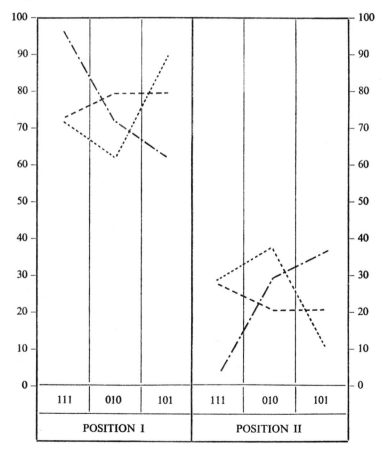

The hypothesis of the present chapter, namely that the predicate assumes position I or II according to whether it can form a typical semantic load pattern or not, seems to break down in the case of pattern 100, the same that in main clauses offered the strongest support for maintaining it. In subordinate clauses light predicates preceded by heavy and followed by light words not only occur in position II, but occur more frequently than in position I, the mean percentages being 65.0 and 34.9. The hypothesis, however, may be regarded as sufficiently supported in the other patterns; moreover, let it be pointed out that even in pattern 100 itself the difference between predicate occurrences in position I and II is expressed in 100% for the main clauses and only 30.2% for the subordinate clauses (the former figure speaks for the hypothesis, the latter against it).

No such discrepancy between the group of main and subordinate clauses exists in the case of pattern 110. The expected equal distribution of predicates in positions I and II actually occurs. The mean proportion is almost perfect, namely 49.9% in position I and 50.1% in position II. If the theoretical assumption, that in this pattern the conflicting tendencies find a balance, is correct, the numbers could hardly give a fuller support to it.

The table on the following page gives an overall picture of predicate distributions in all the patterns.

Examples:

   Position I:

      111: *That Pers preyed Conscience* . . . A, VII, 176;
          . . . and how that freris flowed folke that was . . . B, XIII, 7;
          . . . That freres and monkes token lyflode of luther wynnynges C, XVIII, 35.

      010: *And as I beo-heold in-to the est* . . . A, P, 13;
          wher-of we komen alle B, III, 56;
          . . . that for lawe is seled C, IV, 88.

      110: *That Poul precheth of hem, I dar* . . . A, P, 38;
          . . . as Crist bit hymselue B, XV, 213;
          . . . what Thobie seyde to his wif C, XVIII, 37.

Table Ll

	TEXT A		TEXT B		TEXT C	
	I	II	I	II	I	II
111	1.8% (5)	1.8% (2)	1.9% (14)	1.7% (4)	3.5% (24)	0.3% (1)
010	34.6% (94)	49.5% (56)	27.2% (197)	28.2% (67)	32.6% (220)	28.7% (89)
110	7.7% (21)	19.5% (22)	10.4% (75)	28.7% (68)	10.3% (69)	24.8% (77)
011	6.6% (18)	4.4% (5)	9.9% (72)	0% (—)	15.1% (103)	0% (—)
101	19.5% (53)	6.2% (7)	20.5% (151)	16.9% (40)	13.9% (94)	17.5% (54)
000	4.4% (12)	0% (—)	5.3% (38)	0% (—)	8.8% (59)	4.8% (15)
100	3.7% (10)	15.1% (17)	2.3% (17)	9.7% (23)	1.5% (10)	9.4% (29)
001	21.7% (59)	3.5% (4)	22.5% (164)	14.8% (35)	14.3% (98)	14.5% (45)

011: *Gif I wiste witerly, thou* . . . A, XII, 10;
. . . *tyl I wex wery of the worlde* B, XVIII, 4;
. . . *yf thow coueyte Dowel* C, XII, 142.

101: . . . *with that the pore peple schulde puten in heore wombe* A, III, 75;
. . . *whan his caroigne shal come* B, XII, 254;
. . . *if Holichurche be trewe* C, XVIII, 5.

000: . . . *that I was in a wildernesse* A, P, 12;
. . . *what ioie it was to him* B, XX, 13;
. . . *if thei ben as thei sholde* C, X, 13.

100: . . . *til tho wrecches ben in will* A, XII, 21;
. . . *that the frere wolde for him do more* B, VII, 144;
. . . *the marchante mote nede be lette* C, XIV, 36.

001: . . . *that I wol telle nouthe* A, III, 86;
. . . *as I have lerned in Auynete* B, XII, 257;
. . . *whan he was blynde* C, XVIII, 38.

Position II:

111: ... *that dedly synne or domesday frodyde proude peple* A, IX, 234;
Briddes I bihelde that in buskes made nestes B, XI, 336;
... *yf hus soule come faste* C, XXIII, 300.

010: ... *whon the peple him a-posede with a peny* A, I, 45;
... *that he ne cam fro the pope* B, XIX, 411;
... *that thow ne ruelest rather renkes* C, XIV, 186.

110: *That laborers and louh folk taken of heore maystres, nis* ... A, III, 240;
... *That with-outen wyles leden her lyues* B, XV, 229;
... *til that Kynde* ... *in the myrour of Myddelerde made hym* C, XIV, 132;

011: ... *that he ne worth siker saaf* A, VIII, 55;
(no occurrences in Texts B and C)

101: ... *that here frigthond is hepid* A, III, 234;
... *that Lyf throw his lore shal leue Coueityse* D, XX, 349;
... *that for lawe is seled* C, IV, 88;

000: (no occurrences in texts A and B)
... *that good faithe other-whyle may nat be aspied* C, XXII, 302.

100: ... *that frentik ben of wittes* A, XI, 6;
... *that golde hath to gifte* B, X, 154;
... *til late was and longe* C, VIII, 160.

001: *that I ne schulde maken othur mende* A, III, 53;
... *as he it hath lerned* B, VII, 49;
... *that he ne may louye* C, XX, 327.

2.1.9 It has been demonstrated in sections 2.1.3 and 2.1.6 that the texts of *Piers Plowman* reveal, as one of their characteristic features, numerous predicate occurrences in the end position. It has also been found that the number of heavy predicates in this position is much higher than that of light predicates.

In order to find whether this proportion is characteristic of the predicate only, or whether it is a more general feature of the language as represented by the texts, the following test has been carried out: Two samples of running text were taken from each version of *Piers Plowman,* each containing 100 sentences, and the semantic load of the two words occupying the end position in the sentence was registered. In the count the function of the two words was disregarded, so that predicates were only rarely included.

The test has shown that in a vast majority of sentences a heavy word occupies the final position, the mean proportion of heavy to light words being 73.4% to 26.6%. These figures are comparable to those obtained for the end position of predicates (mean 82.2% to 17.8%) and therefore support the hypothesis that word order patterns are formed within the semantic load patterns. The agreement was less striking if the two last words were compared in the two groups. Pattern 11 was found less frequently in the samples than was expected by analogy to the occurrence of the same pattern with the predicates. The percentages for pattern 10, however, were very close to each other (13.1 for the predicates and 14.3 for the samples). Both in the predicates and in the samples pattern 01 is most abundantly represented (46.2% and 59.0% respectively). It will be noted (cf. Table LII) that the discrepancy between the two values is caused by the subordinate clauses, which may be regarded as a special case, since it is only there that light words in the end position are numerously represented (mean 35.9%). Since in the samples, which include main and subordinate clauses with predicates in the end position as well as main and subordinate clauses not ending with a predicate, heavy words in the final position are found so frequently, and since the relative number of final heavy predicates in the main clauses is even higher, the latter may be said to exhibit the typical tendency most fully, more so than an average sentence, while the subordinate clauses may be regarded as least typical in this respect.

Examples from the portions used for the test:
> 11: *. . . of falsnesse and fastinge and of voues i-broken.* A, P, 68;
> *. . . of al this reume and of al reumes Cristene.* B, XV, 553;
> *. . . as for the grete treuthe.* C, IV, 89.
> 10: *. . . in paradys to playen ther-aftur.* A, VIII, 12;
> *. . . and Fauel and here freres manye!* B, II, 6;
> *. . . hus wif with muche welthe after.* C, XIV, 14.

Table LII

	MAIN CLAUSE MEAN %	SUBORD. CL. MEAN %	MAIN & SUB. MEAN %	SAMPLES MEAN %
11	34.2%	37.9%	36.0%	14.4%
10	0%	26.2%	13.1%	14.3%
01	63.7%	28.6%	46.2%	59.0%
00	2.1%	7.3%	4.7%	12.3%

01: ... *of folk feire I shal ow schewe.* A, I, 2;
    ... *to wonye with wo whil god is in heuene.* B, II, 106;
    ... *yf pacience hym folwe.* C, XIV, 2.
00: ... *heore fauntes euer-more after.* A, VIII, 78;
    ... *and hys consail as clerkus and othere.* C, IV, 151.

2.2 *MIDDLE ENGLISH SERMONS*

2.2.1 In the analysis of the *Middle English Sermons,* as in that of *Piers Plowman,* three positions of the predicate will be distinguished:
  I. Immediate juxtaposition with the subject;
  II. Medial;
  III. Final.

The selection of clauses for the analysis was made in the same way as in the case of *Piers Plowman,* that is, all cases of the predicate-subject order and all those instances of the reverse order, which consist only of the subject and predicate, are included. The number of clauses qualified for the analysis amounted to 6068.

The distribution of predicate occurrences in the three positions in very uneven. Only a small percentage of predicates occurs in positions II and III. The tendency to place the predicate immediately after the subject is so strong that a certain mannerism is noted: If the subject is followed by other words than the predicate, the former is often repeated and put before the latter. Instances like "... *as we see well that osteleres in many places thei will renne"* 85,27; *"Than thei that be lefte, thei rennen to ..."* 86,11, appear in all sermons in great numbers. This being the case, medial and final positions reach only the percentage as shown on the table below.

Table LIII

POSITION	MAIN CLAUSES	SUBORD. CLAUS.
I	97.6% (3116)	96.9% (2798)
II	2.1% (61)	2.0% (57)
III	0.3% (3)	1.1% (33)

Although the percentages for positions I and II are very low indeed, yet it is of interest to compare the cell values of main and subordinate clauses, because of certain analogies to the results as established for *Piers Plowman*. In both texts the difference in the percentage of main and subordinate clauses for position II is very small (0.1% in both), while the difference for position III is large: in *Piers Plowman* the percentage for subordinate clauses is higher than that for main clauses by about one third, in the *Sermons* the proportion is one to four.

Examples:
    Main clauses:
             I: *Trewly Crist loued not vs only in oure prosperite* 93, 22;
            II: *Than anon the frenshippe of is lovers be-for begynneth to with-drawe* 89, 10;
           III: *The more harme is* 18, 8.
    Subordinate clauses:
             I: *... when age suffereth hem no lenger* 236, 14;
            II: *... wherby an vnkende man worthely is punyshed* 287, 20;
           III: *... a beste that vondur is* 77, 11.

2.2.2   When the 01 notations were applied to the predicate and the word standing immediately before it, the distribution of the predicate in the three positions presented a rather confusing picture. In the main clauses pattern 01 received the highest percentages in position I, 11 in position II, and 10 in position III. The fact that pattern 10 reached 100% in position III seems, at first glance, to be in absolute contradiction with the thesis (for which sufficient support was found in *Piers Plowman*) that in the main clauses light predicates avoid the final position. If, however, the problem is approached from a different angle, this proves not to be the case. The 100% is more a negative than a positive result, since end position in general is found very rarely in the *Sermons,* and in main clauses predicates do not assume this position, except for three cases only, and these make the 100%. The number for which the percentage stands is too small to allow any safe conclusions. Similarly the fact that predicate distributions in positions I and II are irregular (as seen on Table LIV), is not yet reason enough to regard the hypothesis as not valid, because in these positions the predicate has one more neighbour, with which it may prove to be matched more favourably (according to the standards established in the analysis of *Piers Plowman*).

In the subordinate clauses the distribution resembles somewhat

Table LIV

	MAIN CLAUSES			SUBORD. CLAUSES		
	I	II	III	I	II	III
11	30.2% (941)	45.9% (28)	0% (—)	18.4% (517)	29.8% (17)	0% (—)
10	3.3% (101)	19.7% (12)	100% (3)	10.8% (302)	47.3% (27)	36.5% (13)
01	41.5% (1299)	34.4% (21)	0% (—)	43.0% (1201)	22.9% (13)	36.5% (12)
00	25.0% (775)	0% (—)	0% (—)	27.8% (778)	0% (—)	27.0% (9)

more closely the "optimal" standard required by the hypothesis: In positions I and II the highest number of occurrences was found with patterns 01 (41.5%) and 10 (47.3%) respectively. Position III also shows a proportion that at least does not speak against the hypothesis, the distribution of predicates in patterns 10 and 01 being equal.

2.2.3 In the preceding section only the word standing immediately before the predicate was taken into consideration. It is now proposed to study the distribution of predicate occurrences in position I and II so that the 01 notations will include the predicate and the word immediately following it.

The hypothesis, that word order patterns are formed within the typical semantic load patterns was hardly supported by the figures obtained from the analysis as described in the preceding section. The situation is entirely different when the predicate is treated as forming a semantic load pattern with the word immediately following it: Pattern 11 is found only in 17.4% in position I and does not occur at all in position II. This agrees with what has been said about the conflicting tendencies: when the semantic load pattern is not typical, the predicate will seek its place in a typical position, that is, immediately after the subject. Hence the discrepancy between positions I and II.

Table LV

	MAIN CLAUSES		SUBORD. CLAUSES	
	I	II	I	II
11	17.4% (540)	0% (—)	7.7% (214)	0% (—)
10	54.6% (1700)	80.3% (49)	53.7% (1504)	52.6% (30)
01	18.0% (562)	0% (—)	29.2% (817)	33.4% (19)
00	10.0% (314)	19.7% (12)	9.4% (263)	14.0% (8)

The high percentage of 10 occurrences in both positions (54.6% and 80.3%) is typical. For the 01 pattern a higher percentage than 18.0 would be expected, if it were not for the fact that in the preceding section the proportion of 01 to 10 was 41.5% to 3.3%. This being the case, the total proportion of 10 to 01 is 57.9% to 59.5%.

The lowest figures were registered for pattern 00.

Full numerical data are presented in Table LV.

2.2.4   In the third stage of the analysis both neighbours of the predicate are taken into consideration and the distribution of the predicate in positions I and II is studied.

Heavy predicates with heavy words on both sides were found very rarely. Since all instances of 111 were found in position I, it is concluded that the situation in the *Sermons* is analogous to that in *Piers Plowman,* that is, in the non-typical semantic load pattern predicates assume, or tend to assume, the typical position, namely immediately after their subjects.

In position I the highest percentage was registered for pattern 010, the next highest for 110; in position II the order is a reverse one. In both, however, the two patterns contain more instances than any other configuration, and may therefore be regarded as the typical patterns for the *Sermons*.

Unexpectedly low is the percentage of pattern 101, especially in the main clauses. In the subordinate clauses this configuration reaches a higher percentage, namely 10.5 in position I and 33.3 in position II. At first glance this proportion seems to disprove the thesis that the subject tends to attract its predicate not only in the case of a non-typical semantic load pattern, but first of all when that pattern is favourable. However, a comparison of the absolute numbers reveals that this is not so. The number of light predicates surrounded by two heavy words amounts to 295 in position I, and is only 19 in position II, that is, the light predicate is found in immediate juxtaposition with its heavy subject in 94.0%, while only in 6.0% of all the cases of pattern 101 the predicate is separated from its subject.

It has been said above that patterns 010 and 110 are most typical for the text, pattern 111 least typical. It has also been pointed out that the predicate tends to avoid a position which is non-typical in a double way. The basis for such a statement provided the differences in frequencies of predicate occurrences in I — 111, 101, 010 on the one hand, and in II — 111, 101, 010 on the other. The data from the *Middle English Sermons* can be compared with those from *Piers Plowman* and close similarities are found.

Table LVI

	MAIN CLAUSES		SUBORD. CLAUSES	
	III	II	I	II
111	100% (178)	0% (—)	100% (24)	0% (—)
010	97.5% (937)	2.5% (21)	98.8% (1011)	1.2% (13)
101	100% (92)	0% (—)	94.0% (295)	6.0% (19)

The non-typical 111 pattern does not occur in position II; the typical 010 and 101 patterns have at least some occurrences in that position, whereby the comparatively high percentage of the latter in subordinate clauses compensates for the lack of occurrences in main clauses. Although the numbers are small, their overall distribution in the cells is regular enough and perhaps they can be used as support for the theoretical formula that the predicate will tend more strongly to join the subject when the alternative position does not offer a favourable semantic load pattern, than when the reverse is the case.

Examples:
　Main clauses, position I:
　　　111: *Loo, sirs, perfite techynge elumynethe mans soule* 242, 10;
　　　010: *Inys moders vombe he ioyed for the commynge* 93, 11;

101: *Thise iij maries ben exsampled to all* ... 135, 7.
Main clauses, position II:
  111: (no occurrences)
  010: *Ther euery man than taketh of othur* ... 86, 8;
  101: (no occurrences)
Subordinate clauses, position I:
  111: ... *when age suffreth lenger to do* ... 301, 30;
  010: ... *that thou maketh thi-selfe thorowe* 108, 11;
  101: *by whos ligte men mygthe rise from* ... 237, 18;
Subordinate clauses, position II:
  111: (no occurrences)
  010: ... *how it hym maketh to com vn-to the blis* 49, 30;
  101: ... *whereby that a vnkende man may worthely be pu-nyshed* 31, 17.

The following table shows the distribution of predicate occurrences in all the patterns.

Table LVII

	MAIN CLAUSES		SUBORD. CLAUSES	
	I	II	I	II
111	5.7% (178)	0% (—)	0.9% (24)	0% (—)
010	30.1% (937)	34.4% (21)	36.1% (1011)	22.9% (13)
110	24.5% (763)	46.0% (28)	17.6% (493)	29.8% (17)
011	11.6% (362)	0% (—)	6.8% (190)	0% (—)
101	2.9% (92)	0% (—)	10.5% (295)	33.3% (19)
000	9.8% (305)	0% (—)	9.1% (256)	0% (—)
100	0.3% (9)	19.6% (12)	0.2% (7)	14.0% (8)
001	15.1% (470)	0% (—)	18.8% (522)	0% (—)

2.2.5 In the *Sermons* end position of predicates occurs, unlike in *Piers Plowman,* chiefly with light predicates. In order to find whether a word having light semantic load is typical for the end position in general, two samples from different parts of the text, each containing 100 sentences, were tested for the semantic load of the last word in the sentence.

It was found that in the majority of sentences the last word had a heavy semantic load. The figures 76.0% and 24.0% are strikingly similar to those obtained in an analogous test in *Piers Plowman.* However, in the *Sermons* these percentages do not match those reflected in the distribution of light and heavy predicates in the final position, where the proportion is a reverse one (86.7% and 13.3%). This result was modified when the last two words were compared. The discrepancy proved to be not one of the opposition of light and heavy word, but of pattern 10 and 01. As can be seen on table LVIII, the proportion of 10 to 01 in the predicates is roughly the reverse of the proportion of the samples.

It is concluded that predicates in the final position do not show the typical semantic load patterns found elsewhere in the texts of the *Sermons.*

Table LVIII

	MAIN CLAUSES	SUBORD. CLAUSES	MEAN OF MAIN SUB.	MEAN OF SAMPLES
11	0%	0%	0%	16.4%
10	100%	36.5%	68.3%	13.0%
01	0%	36.5%	13.3%	59.6%
00	0%	27.0%	13.5%	11.0%

Examples from the portion used for the test:
11: . . . *as redely to ys grace as a good doer.* 163, 2;
     . . . *giff he will baske forgeuenes.* 165, 7;
10: *He receyveth nowe.* 163, 16;
     He seith thus: 265, 30;
01: . . . *to seye on English to youre vndirstondynge.* 162, 24;
     . . . *of a shippe in the middes of the see.* 266, 7;
00: . . . *with is neygbore is euell at ease with hymself.* 264, 1;
     . . . *at the on ere and goyth oute at the othur.* 166, 23.

2.3 SUMMARY

The most typical position for the predicate is the first place
after the subject. The two other positions (medial and final —
the latter occurring more frequently in subordinate than in main
clauses) are found less often in *Piers Plowman,* and very rarely
in the *Sermons.* The relation of the three positions to the typical
and non-typical semantic load patterns leads to the conclusion
that the predicate assumes one of the three positions to give way
to the tendency to form typical "rhythmic" structures, which are
identical in both texts and go beyond the predicate and its neighbours. Patterns, in which elements of unequal semantic load are
matched, are most typical everywhere except in clause-final positions. The tendency to end the clause with a heavy word is so
strong, that not infrequently the otherwise non-typical 11 pattern
reaches a higher percentage than 01. In the *Sermons,* however,
light predicates occur even in final positions. This, and the lower
proportion of medial and final positions in general, constitute the
only major differences between *Piers Plowman* and *Middle
English Sermons.*

3. THE POSITION OF THE OBJECT

3.1 *PIERS PLOWMAN*

3.1.1 The present study deals only with those objects which are part of the subject-predicate construction. Objects belonging to a predicate that refers to a subject expressed in a preceding clause are also included. Excluded, however, are all instances of objects with a dative construction, like *Moche wonder me thynketh* B, XV, 372; *Me liketh wel gowre wordes* B, I, 43. Objects of infinitives (e.g. *To breke beggeris bred* A, XI, 185) as well as those belonging to a construction where the subject is repeated (e.g. *Seriauntes for here seruise mede they asken* C, IV, 274) are are also excluded. Finally, the present study will not deal with instances where it is impossible to regard one particular word as the object proper. This is the case with phrases or whole clauses in the function of an object.

In the course of the analysis it became evident that the position of the object in main and subordinate clauses was basically identical, and therefore no such distinction will be made in the present chapter.

The number of objects, to which the present study refers, amounts to 1621 in Text A, 4801 in Text B, and 5213 in Text C. By far the greatest proportion of objects was found with constructions where the predicate follows the subject, the second largest group is that where the object belongs to a predicate referring to a subject expressed in a preceding clause. The smallest number of instances was found in the predicate-subject sequences. If S means subject, P predicate, and X object, the distribution of objects in the three texts of *Piers Plowman* is:

I. X with SP: Text A: 1018
            Text B: 3034
            Text C: 3255
            TOTAL : 7307

II. X with PS: Text A: 59
            Text B: 173
            Text C: 312
            TOTAL : 544

III. X with P : Text A: 554
            Text B: 1594
            Text C: 1646
            TOTAL : 3794

In groups I and II there exist three possibilities in which the elements in question can be arranged, in group III two possibilities. All these possible configurations are represented in the texts, but their frequency of occurrence differs considerably, as seen on the table below.

Table LIX [1]

SPX	SXP	XSP
51.7% (6046)	10.1% (1185)	0.7% (76)

PSX	PXS	XPS
2.1% (250)	0% (1)	2.5% (293)

PX	XP
31.4% (3673)	1.0% (121)

[1] Each of the three words can, of course, have other words as immediate neighbours. Here, however, only their succession is taken into consideration, since the problem of surroundings of the object will be discussed separately.

The various configurations will be dealt with separately and due attention will be paid to the fluctuations between the texts of *Piers Plowman* in the following sections.

3.1.2 The percentage of SPX, as compared with the numbers for SXP and XSP, reaches the figure 82.6. This sequence, then, may be regarded as the typical order for the texts. SXP and XSP are represented by 16.1% and 1.3% respectively, and are treated as non-typical configurations. The three sequences are distributed in the three texts of *Piers Plowman* with only little fluctuation, as seen on the table below.

Table LX

TEXT	SPX	SXP	XSP
A	83.2% (848)	15.8% (160)	1.0% (10)
B	83.0% (2522)	16.1% (483)	0.9% (29)
C	82.2% (2676)	16.7% (542)	1.1% (37)

3.1.3 In sequences where the subject follows the predicate, the object can, theoretically, also assume three positions. In Texts B and C, however, it never occurs between the predicate and the subject, and in Text A only one instance was found. This very definitely suggests the non-typical character of the PXS pattern. The proportion of the other two configurations is 46.0% to 53.8%, the latter number representing the XPS pattern. In the non-typical predicate-subject order, then, the object occupies a non-typical position from the point of view of the subject-predicate order. This is in agreement with the data collected in chapter 1, where it was observed that, if the prepositional is an object, it is more often followed by the predicate-subject than the subject-predicate order. Since the calculations for determining the influence of the prepositional on the relation of subject to predicate were based on all the object occurrences, and the differences between the percentages of XPS and XSP were more pronounced, the small discrepancy between the percentages of the same patterns in the present chapter (7.8%) may be ascribed to the need of restricting the present study of object occurrences to only those instances where a particular word can be treated as the object proper. For this reason it is suggested to regard the XPS order as the typical pattern in the predicate-subject group, in spite of the difficulty as presented by Text A, where the PSX sequence occurs more often than XPS.

Table LXI

	TEXT A	TEXT B	TEXT C
PSX	57.6% (34)	43.3% (75)	45.2% (141)
PXS	1.7% (1)	0% (—)	0% (—)
XPS	40.7% (24)	56.7% (98)	54.8% (171)

3.1.4   In the group of predicates referring to a subject expressed in another clause, the picture is very clear. The object is found to follow the predicate in almost all cases. The differences between the three texts do not excede 0.3%.

Table LXII

	TEXT A	TEXT B	TEXT C
PX	96.5% (535)	97.0% (1546)	96.8% (1592)
XP	3.5% (19)	3.0% (48)	3.2% (54)

Examples:
  X with SP:
    SPX: *I grette the gode mon* A, XI, 167;
      I suffre gou no lengere B, IV, 1;
      Ich haue ywedded a wyf C, VIII, 300.

SXP: ... *as the gode wyf me taugte* A, XI, 167;
    ... *as telleth this poetes* B, XII, 237;
    For he no monye weldeth C, XXIII, 12.

XSP: *That Poul preceth of hem* A, P, 38;
    The peple thow lernest B, XIII, 72;
    Pers ich wille folwen C, XI, 51.

X with PS:

  PSX: *For culde I neuere no kyng* A, III, 180;
      Shal no greyne that groweth glade gow at nede B,
      VI, 121;
      With-oute gult ... gat ich thys scathe C, V, 75.

  PXS: ... *so berith witnesse the sauter* A, XI, 189;
      (no occurrences in Texts B and C)

  XPS: *Coure gates wilde I holden* A, XII, 88;
      Al this seig I slepyng B, P, 230;
      And that seeth the saule C, II, 39.

X with P:

    PX: *Al the pore peple pese-coddes fetten, bake benes in
       bred* A, VII, 280;
       *Pore men thow robbedest, and bere here bras at the
       bakke* B, III, 195;
       ... *monye mad hym meny frendes ... and rendreth
       hus byble* C, XI, 88.

    XP: ... *men, that here foode haue* A, VII, 57;
       She leteth passe prisoneres ... that harme dede B,
       III, 140;
       Prestes that prechen and the puple techen C, IV, 279.

The graph on the following page summarizes the results of sections
3.1.2–3.1.4.

3.1.5   It is now proposed to study the subject-predicate-object
relations with regard to the semantic load patterns the object
forms with the subject or predicate, or both.

In the SPX sequence the object follows its predicate immediately in 2977 cases. No instance of the 00 pattern was found.
The percentages for the remaining patterns are:

$$11 \ — \ 30.5$$
$$01 \ — \ \ 6.8$$
$$10 \ — \ 62.7$$

Table LXIII

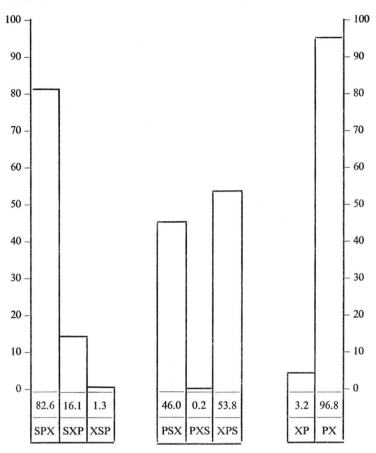

82.6	16.1	1.3		46.0	0.2	53.8		3.2	96.8
SPX	SXP	XSP		PSX	PXS	XPS		XP	PX

This is in apparent contradiction with what has been so far claimed about the typical semantic load patterns. Not only is the proportion of 10 to 01 unexpected, but the frequency of 11 is too high for a non-typical pattern. In spite of this, however, it is maintained that the hypothesis concerning semantic load patterns is not disproved by the above figures, and that for two reasons, one of which will be given in the present section.[2]

---

[2] The second reason is given in the next section.

Although it is true that the number of instances in the 11 pattern is very high, yet not in all the instances is pattern 11 non-typical, because out of the number of 906 cases where the object forms this pattern with the predicate, it is the last word of the clause in 335 cases, where, as has been shown in the preceding chapter, this pattern is most typical. Although the following table includes all the instances of the pattern in question, 37.0% of them should be regarded as typical.

Table LXIV

	TEXT A	TEXT B	TEXT C
11	30.4% (117)	27.8% (325)	32.5% (464)
10	68.3% ʼ383)	65.4% (1166)	59.3% (1428)
01	1.3% (5)	6.8% (79)	8.2% (118)

The distribution is totally different in the XSP sequence. Out of the 72 instances where the object is in immediate juxtaposition with the subject, not a single case constitutes the 11 pattern. The typical 01 and 10 patterns include all cases except one, which forms pattern 00.

It has been shown in section 3.1.2 that the SPX sequence is doubtlessly the typical one (82.6%), XSP the least typical (0.2%). If this is compared with the figures just mentioned, it is possible to conclude the following: Since in the non-typical sequence no cases of non-typical semantic load patterns are found, while in the typical sequence their number is high, and conversely, since in the non-typical sequence the prevalence of the typical semantic load pattern is especially striking,[3] it is possible

---

[3] If it were not for the one case of 000 pattern, of XSP could be said to be formed exclusively in typical semantic load patterns. It will be remembered, however, that pattern 00 does not necessarily mean two elements of equal semantic load.

that the function of the XSP sequence is to balance the distribution of semantic load patterns. More of it will be said below.

Table LXV

	TEXT A	TEXT B	TEXT C
11	—	—	—
10	71.4% (5)	71.4% (20)	70.2% (26)
01	28.6% (2)	25.0% (7)	29.8% (11)
00	—	3.6% (1)	—

If sequence SPX is the most and sequence XSP the least typical one, and if the above statement is correct, it would be expected that SXP, which stands somewhere between the two extrems, should reveal a corresponding distribution of semantic load pattern. This is actually the case in Texts A and B, where the occurrence of the pattern, in which elements of equal semantic load are matched, is lower than 30.5% (SPX), but higher than 0,2% (XSP). Only in Text C is the percentage of the non-typical pattern higher than 30.5%.

Table LXVI

	TEXT A	TEXT B	TEXT C
111	22.4% (26)	26.3% (89)	36.6% (118)
010	2.6% (3)	8.6% (29)	9.0% (29)
110	0% (—)	7.4% (25)	5.3% (17)
101	75.0% (87)	57.5% (195)	49.1% (158)

(other patterns do not occur)

On three graphs, each representing one word order pattern, the correlation between that pattern and the semantic load pattern can be seen clearly. In the typical word order the discrepancy between typical and non-typical semantic load patterns is smallest, in the non-typical order the discrepancy is highest; in both the differences between the texts are slight. In the word order which is neither typical nor non-typical, the extreme points of the neighbouring graphs are not reached; moreover, the differences between the three texts are considerable.

Table LXVII

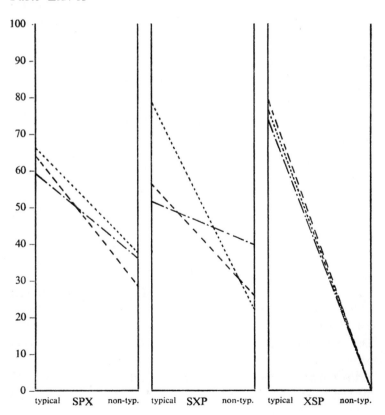

3.1.6 In predicate-subject sequences objects occur less frequently. In the PSX order the object is never found in immediate juxtaposition with the subject, in the PXS order it follows the predicate immediately only in one instance, forming the 11 pattern with the predicate. If this is negative evidence for the hypothesis stated in the preceding section, positive evidence is provided by the distribution of semantic load patterns in the XPS sequence. As in the subject-predicate sequence, if the object heads the construction, it is never found in such an immediate contact with the predicate that a non-typical semantic load pattern would be the result. On the contrary, it forms a typical semantic load with the subject in 91.2% of all the instances, 8.8% being found in the 00 pattern. Although the numbers on which the percentages are calculated are small, the proportions between them are pronounced enough to be of use in supporting the hypothesis.

Table LXVIII

	TEXT A	TEXT B	TEXT C
11	0% (—)	0% (—)	0% (—)
10	77.8% (14)	85.0% (73)	87.0% (127)
01	11.1% (2)	7.5% (6)	3.4% (5)
00	11.1% (2)	7.5% (6)	9.6% (14)

3.1.7 Objects of predicates referring to subjects of another clause show a comparable distribution of semantic load patterns in PX and XP sequences. The former includes 1472 instances, out of which 577 objects form a 11 pattern with the predicates. This percentage (39.6), although lower than that of the typical pattern (60.1), can be accounted for by the fact that it is found in the typical sequence, which seems to enforce that pattern. In the non-typical XP this force is not active at all, and it is expected that no instances of the non-typical pattern, or only very few, will be found. That this is so can be seen on table LXX.

Table LXIX

	TEXT A	TEXT B	TEXT C
11	34.8% (80)	39.5% (238)	40.5 (259)
10	59.5% (136)	54.5% (329)	48.9% (313)
01	5.7% (13)	6.0% (36)	9.8% (63)
00	0% (—)	0% (—)	0.8% (5)

Table LXX

	TEXT A	TEXT B	TEXT C
11	15.8% (3)	0% (—)	0% (—)
10	68.4% (13)	75.0% (42)	74.0% (40)
01	15.8% (3)	25.0% (14)	26.0% (14)
00	0% (—)	0% (—)	0% (—)

3.1.8 Sections 3.1.5 to 3.1.7 have provided material for a hypothesis that can be formulated in the following way: Since the semantic load of the subject, predicate and object in a given sequence is determined by the objective situation, and since in the typical word order configurations (as established in sections 3.1.2 to 3.1.4) a high percentage of non-typical semantic load patterns is found, while the non-typical word order configurations contain very few such instances, it is claimed that the presence of the non-typical word order configurations is dictated by the tendency to a proportionate distribution of semantic load patterns.

3.1.9   The study of the correlation of word order and semantic load patterns included so far only instances in which the object stood in immediate juxtaposition with the subject or predicate. Very often, however, one or more words separate it from the subject or predicate. In this way the object is found to form semantic load patterns with its neighbours other than the subject and predicate. It is proposed to study these relations in the present section.

The subject-predicate sequence offers the following combinations:

SP . . . X
S . . . XP
X . . . SP
SX . . . P
S . . . X . . . P

In the texts, however, only the first three occur. Neither are all semantic load patterns represented, as seen on the tables below. Since only four instances of X . . . SP were found, the figures presented on table LXXIII will not be used for the sake of any argument.

If Table LXXI is compared with Table LXIV, it will be noticed that the percentage of the non-typical pattern is smaller in the former. An even more marked difference will be observed in the case of Tables LXVI and LXXII. This being the situation, it seems possible to extend the hypothesis stated in section 3.1.8 by saying that the object very often finds a favourable semantic load pattern by simply moving away from the immediate neighbourhood with the subject or predicate. In this way no "violence" is done to the typical subject-predicate-object sequence. A point in favour of this suggestion is the fact that the absolute number of SP . . . X occurrences is much greater than that of the less typical S . . . XP and the non-typical X . . . SP sequence, where by moving the object farther away nothing is gained for the typical character of the sequence.

Table LXXI

	TEXT A	TEXT B	TEXT C
11	23.3% (83)	13.3% (135)	20.4% (183)
10	24.2% (86)	22.9% (233)	22.9% (205)
01	52.5% (187)	63.8% (648)	56.7% (508)
00	no occurrences		

Table LXXII

	TEXT A	TEXT B	TEXT C
111	no occurrences		
010	4.5% (2)	14.5% (21)	26.0% (57)
011	95.5% (42)	85.5% (123)	64.5% (142)
110	0% (—)	0% (—)	9.5% (21)
000, 101, 001, 100-no occurrences			

Table LXXIII

	TEXT A	TEXT B	TEXT C
11	33.3% (1)	0% (—)	0% (—)
10	66.7% (2)	100% (1)	0% (—)
10,00 - no occurrences			

3.1.10   In the predicate-subject sequence only X ... PS will be considered in some detail, as P ... XS and P ... X ... S are not represented in the texts at all, and PS ... X and PX ... S have no corresponding occurrences in PSX and PXS; moreover, the number of instances in these groups is too small to be of use for possible conclusions. It is enough to state that all instances form either the 110 or the 100 pattern.

The distribution of semantic load patterns in X ... PS is: 11 — 29.6%, 10 — 63.6%, and 01 — 6.8%. If X ... PS were a typical sequence, the comparatively high proportion of the non-typical pattern would speak against the amplification of the hypothesis as stated in the preceding section. Since the reverse is the case, the figures support it. Full data are presented in the following table.

Table LXXIV

	TEXT A	TEXT B	TEXT C
11	33.3% (2)	30.8% (4)	28.0% (7)
10	50.0% (3)	69.2% (9)	64.0% (16)
01	16.7% (1)	0% (—)	8.0% (2)

3.1.11   P ... X, as opposed to X ... P, is a typical sequence. It is expected that in the former the number of 11 instances will be smaller than in PX, and also that the typical semantic load patterns will occur with higher frequency. This expectation meets the facts. The mean percentage for pattern 11 was as high as 39.6 in the typical sequence (compare table LXVIII), while in P ... X no instances of 11 are found. The numbers for the typical pattern also seem to support the amplified hypothesis: Pattern 01 is the only one found in this sequence.

Only two cases of X ... P have been found, and they both form pattern 01.

Examples: [4]

111: ... *whan Pilat a-posed god almygti* A, XII, 26;
      The pope and alle prelatis presentz vnderfongen B, III, 214;
      May no kynge mercy graunt C, XX, 285;

010: *Peni-ale and piriwiht heo pourede to-geder* A, V, 134;
      And when ich loue leelly oure lord and ... C, XVII, 195.

011: ... *that Wrong for his werkes schulde wo thole* A, IV, 71;
      ... *men by olde tyme ensamples token and termen* B, XII, 237;
      And Pers thorgh pacience alle pereles stoppede C, XXI, 462.

110: *Thenne gon I meten a meruelous sweuene* A, P, 11;
      Alkynnes crafty men crauen mede for here prentis B, III, 224;
      Prestes ... *asken mede and masse-pans* C, IV, 280.

000: *That can I the wisse* A, XI, 228;
      For al this I haue hated in myne herte B, V, 71;
      Al this haue we seyn C, IV, 104.

101: *And thou hast famed me foule* A, III, 179;
      ... *as telleth this poetes* B, XII, 237;
      ... *ther al resun hym dampneth* C, XX, 283.

001: *Al this saug I slepynge* A, P, 109;
      ... *alle thise late I passe* B, V, 416;
      And that knoweth Conscience C, IV, 225.

100: *I my-seluen haue i-founded hem furst folk to deceyue* A, XI, 161;
      His wif gan edwite hym tho B, V, 370;
      Neode nymeth hym a-non vnder hus mayn-pryse C, XXIII, 17.

3.1.12   Object occurrences in inital and final positions show an interesting distribution of semantic load patterns, and one that seems to provide evidence for the main thesis of the present study.

It has been established in chapter I that in initial positions pattern 11 occurs very rarely, while pattern 01 is found most frequently, and next to it pattern 10. This general proportion

---

[4]   By grouping the examples according to patterns consisting of three symbols, a fuller picture of the variety of patterns is given. The symbol in the middle stands for the object.

is preserved on a microscopic scale in initial object occurrences. The following numerical data show the distribution in detail.

Table LXXV

11	10	01	00
1.7% (1)	13.3% (8)	83.3% (50)	1.7% (1)

Even more satisfactory results, because based on a larger number of instances, have been achieved in the analysis of objects in final positions. Chapter 2 in general and the sample test in particular provided figures to the effect that pattern 11, which occurs very rarely in initial positions, is found more often when final, but even in this position the prevailing pattern is 01. With this in mind, one would expect the percentage of 11 patterns, which the object forms in final positions, at least to excede the 1.7% of 11 patterns in initial positions. Not only is this expectation confirmed, but the percentages of the particular patterns formed by the object and its neighbour (Table LXXVI) compare well with the percentages obtained in the test (Table LII). In no pattern, except 00, is the difference larger than 8.5%. This agreement between the "microscopic" and the "macroscopic" percentages once more points to the validity of the main argument of the study, that word order can be treated as dependent on the semantic load patterns.

Table LXXVI

11	10	01	00
21.8% (590)	10.2% (276)	67.5% (1826)	0.5% (13)

3.2 *MIDDLE ENGLISH SERMONS*

3.2.1 As in the case of *Piers Plowman,* a number of object occurrences, which have not been thought suitable for the purpose of the present study, have been left out of consideration. The largest group of the rejected instances constitute clauses and phrases, because of the impossibility to regard one particular word as the object proper (e.g. *he saw howe faire she was in soule* 331,21). Objects of dative constructions as well as objects of infinitives (e.g. *to informe the in the right feythe* 127,8) are also excluded.

The present sections refer to 3628 instances of object occurrences. Analogously to *Piers Plowman,* in the *Middle English Sermons* by far the largest number of objects was found with the subject-predicate construction, and in these the object precedes both subject and predicate only in a small minority of cases, while it is never found between the subject and predicate. The second largest group are objects after a predicate whose subject is expressed in another clause. No object-predicate sequences occur. With the predicate-subject construction objects are found very rarely, and when found, the latter occupy a position after both predicate and subject, never between the two, and comparatively infrequently before them. The following table shows to what extent the theoretically possible sequences are used in the texts of the *Sermons.*

Table LXXVII

SPX	SXP	XSP		PSX	PXS	XPS
68.0% (2464)	0% (—)	1.8% (65)		5.2% (192)	0% (—)	1.2% (44)

PX	XP
23.8% (863)	0% (—)

Examples:

SPX: *And ther-for when that he tempteth vs to do ill* 142, 23;
XSP: *This name man taketh firste* 108, 35;
PSX: *Serue ge God in drede* 35, 9;
XPS: *Figure and liknes haue we here-of* 216, 14;
PX: *. . . and thei that vndirstode amysse the lawe of Criste* 2, 8.

From the above figures it follows that the object almost regularly assumes the typical position, that is, a place after the subject and predicate, or after the predicate in case of group III. Even in the predicate-subject order it is more often placed after than before the two. However, while the proportion of SPX to XSP is 97.7 to 2.3, that of PSX to XPS is 80.5 to 19.5. This difference is due to the tendency (described in Chapter 1) to the predicate-subject order after the prepositional.

3.2.2   The analysis of the position of the object in *Piers Plowman* led to the conclusion that the presence of the non-typical order is, at least to some extent, dictated by the need to arrange words into groups so that typical semantic load patterns will be formed. The *Middle English Sermons* seem to provide material which would support this hypothesis from a negative angle. The absence of SXP and PSX sequences, and the much lower (as compared with *Piers Plowman*) occurrence of XSP and XPS coincides with a complete absence of the non-typical semantic load pattern in the remaining sequences, because invariably at least one immediate neighbour of the object has a different semantic load pattern than it itself possesses. It is concluded that since, for whatever reason,[5] the language of the *Sermons* manages to avoid patterns 11 and 111 in the neighbourhood of the object, there is no need for non-typical word order that would balance the distribution of semantic load patterns.

    [5]   One of the reasons might be a higher proportion of light verbs, which is a consequence of the development of compound tenses. Also it is not impossible that the character of the literary document enforces a higher frequency of pronouns (especially the second person, since the priest addresses the congregation). The problem, however, is not investigated here, as it lies outside the scope and the method of the present study.

It was also stated in connection with *Piers Plowman* that very often the object does not change its position, but simply shifts away from the subject or predicate in order to find a favourable semantic load configuration with the other members of the sequence. Since in the *Sermons* no 11 patterns occur with the object, there would seem to be no reason for the great number of objects which are found separated from their predicates. However, a comparison of SPX and PX on the one hand and SP . . . X and P . . . X on the other suggests a solution that follows the same lines as those which were found valid for *Piers Plowman*. In the most typical semantic load patterns, namely 010 and 101, the number of instances is much higher when the object is separated from the predicate than when it occupies the first place after it, the proportions being 85.5% to 14.5% for 010, and 62.6% tot 37.4% for 101. Even more striking is the situation in the case of objects following a predicate that refers to a subject expressed in another clause. The object never forms pattern 010 with the predicate itself, while in the P . . . X sequence as many as 370 instances were found.[6] Similar, though less obvious proportions are provided by the less typical patterns.

The following table presents the distribution of semantic load patterns in the whole text.

Table LXXVIII

PATT.	PERC.	PATT.	PERC.
111	0 (—)	000	1.7 (43)
010	39.7 (1000)	101	10.5 (264)
011	5.2 (131)	001	1.3 (32)
110	22.9 (576)	100	18.7 (470)

[6] With pattern 101, however, P . . . X does not occur at all.

3.2.3   The statement about the non-occurrence of pattern 11 referred only to cases where the object is not the last word in the clause, because in this position objects with heavy semantic load are actually found in immediate juxtaposition with either a heavy predicate or another heavy word. The distribution of semantic load patterns which the object forms in an end position is given in the table below.

Table LXXIX

11	10	01	00
23.6% (263)	45.2% (502)	30.7% (341)	0.5% (6)

If the "microscopic" distribution of semantic load patterns in end positions (objects) is compared with the "macroscopic" distribution (end position in general), it is found that the agreement is very close, the proportions of the typical patterns to 11 being 75.9% to 23.6% for the objects, and 72.6% to 16.4% for end positions in general. This shows that the object obeys the general rules regarding the distribution of semantic load patterns. If it is added that the proportion of SPX to SP...X is 79.5% to 20.5%, the hypothesis that the object gives up immediate neighbourhood with its predicate in order to contribute to a balanced distribution of semantic load patterns, seems to have received necessary support.

Examples:
     111:   (no occurrences)
     010:   ... *ne I will no thinge do* 142, 28;
     011:   ... *the same wordes Crist rerherseth* 52, 20;
     110:   *Seynt Petre founde Seynt Clement of so good liff* 7.1;
     000:   ... *and ther-fore biddeth the prophete thise too togethur* 35, 8;
     101:   *The emperour held hym ascused* 158, 12;
     001:   ... *that oweth the an hundred pens* 37, 10;
     100:   ... *that he will this day refreshe me in connynge* 189, 21.

3.3 SUMMARY

The subject-predicate-object sequence is typical for both texts. In the predicate-subject order the object (especially in *Piers Plowman*) often precedes both subject and predicate. Non-typical positions of the object occur chiefly in *Piers Plowman*.

A correlation between the position of the object and the semantic load patterns has been established. Since objects always (or almost always) form typical semantic load patterns in non-typical positions, while in the typical position a high percentage of non-typical semantic load patterns is found, the presence of the non-typical order may be treated as giving the object a possibility of finding suitable surroundings. The almost complete absence of non-typical orders in the *Sermons,* together with the fact that even the typical order has always a typical semantic load pattern, may be regarded as negative evidence in support of the hypothesis. The tendency to form typical semantic load patterns also seems to account for the fact that objects are often found at some distance from their predicates.

4. HISTORICAL ASPECT

4.1   The fourteenth century, which produced the texts under scrutiny, is said to be a period of transition in the field of word order, as in other fields. That this is so can be seen in the graphs below, which summarize the development of certain characteristic features of word order, which – step by step – become less frequent, until they disappear almost completely from some Middle English texts, and are present in a much smaller proportion in others.

4.2   There is, however, one feature that does not seem to keep pace with historical development and shows signs of stability through many centuries, reaching apparently as far back as the period of West Germanic Unity. The feature in question is the semantic load patterning.

In a study of *Heliand* John Ries had established what he called "rhythmic laws"; they are three in number:
1. Das Gesetz vom Satzauftakt,
2. Das Gesetz der ersten Senkung,
3. Das Gesetz vom Satzschluss.[1]

Since the first law means "Proklise an den ersten Hochton", the second "Enklise an die erste Haupthebung", and the third says that "tonschwache Worte die letzte Stelle im Satze meiden",[2] they are equivalents (only limited to initial and final positions in the sentence) of what in the present study received treatment as semantic load patterns (in a broader application). The definitions differ, but the results are identical. The first two laws correspond to patterns 01 and 10 respectively, the third to patterns 01 and 11 occurring in clause-final positions in the texts

[1]   Ries, *Heliand*, p. 33 ff.
[2]   *Ibid.*, p. 34.

presently analyzed. Ries's laws do not have any absolute character, but rather express a tendency, and this is fully compatible with the result of the present study. 01 and 10 patterns were indeed found more frequently (though not only in initial position) than any other pattern, and patterns 01 and 11 were also found typical for final positions in both texts.

That these laws hold good for *Beowulf* has been conclusively shown by Ries.[3] But even at a much later time, when word order has already approached the patterns of present day English, at least traces of it remain, as certain hints from various scholars seem to suggest. Chaucer's *Melibeus* and *The Person's Tale* may be quoted as examples from the same period as *Piers Plowman* and *Middle English Sermons*. Heussler[4] states that the predicate-subject order is usually found when it is preceded by an adverb, especially *then*. This statement could be put into: inversion takes place when a word with light semantic load stands at the beginning of the sentence. Although no statistical data are included in his study, some statements seem to suggest that inversion does not occur with a nominal subject and a light predicate.

Another hint is given in a study of a much later text, namely that of Buyan. Snoek[5] says that "bei Bunyan findet sich dieser Gebrauch (predicate-subject order) nur noch zu Anfang der Rede bei den Verben des Sagens und des Meinens, die schon im Ae. in diesem Falle zur Inversion neigen". Since a pronominal subject is practically the rule with verbs of "Sagen und Meinen", this simply means that even in a seventeenth century text the non-typical word order pattern, when it occurs, is formed within a semantic load pattern, which had remained typical for such a long period.

4.3 A comparison of statistical data drawn from studies pertaining to ancient English texts shows a clear developing line.

---

[3] Ries, *Beowulf*, pp. 73, 91, 114.
[4] Heussler, *Chaucer's Melibeus*, p. 10.
[5] Snoek, *Bunyan*, p. 25.

Although even in *Beowulf* the subject-predicate order is found more often than the predicate-subject order, the frequency of the former tends to rise as centuries go by, the increase between the eight and the fourteenth century being 27.2%.

Another characteristic feature of ancient English word order is the high frequency of predicate occurrences in final positions in the sentence, whereby the frequency is higher in subordinate than in main clauses. This feature also tends to disappear in the course of history, the difference in percentage between the eigth and the fourteenth century being 68.9 for main and 85.1 for subordinate clauses. It is interesting to note that in no period

Table LXXX

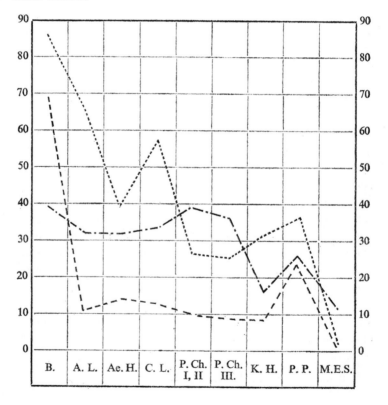

does the proportion of final predicates in main clauses transcend that of final predicates in subordinate clauses.

In the graph on p. 106 - . - . - . - shows the decrease of predicate-subject occurrences, - - - - - and ...... the decrease of final predicate occurrences in main and subordinate clauses respectively. (Symbols used: B. – Beowulf, A.L. – Alfred's Laws, Ae.H. – Aelfric's Homilies, C.L. – Cnut's Laws, P.Ch. – Peterborough Chronicles, K.H. – King Horn, P.P. – Piers Plowman, M.E.S. – Middle English Sermons.)

It will be noticed that the decrease in the occurrence of the three features is not exactly parallel: The particular texts are more advanced in one aspect, less so in another. Thus *Cnut's Laws* show a somewhat high percentage of final predicate occurrences in subordinate clauses, the *Peterborough Chronicles* in predicate-subject occurrences, *Piers Plowman* of all three features. *Middle English Sermons* seem to be most "regular". Unfortunately no statistical data for Chaucer and other fourteenth century writers are available. From the general statements contained in Heuss-

Table LXXXI

TEXT	PS	FINAL PRED. MAIN CL.	FINAL PRED. SUBORD. CL.
Beowulf	38.2%	69.2%	86.2%
Alfred	32.7%	11.0%	65.1%
Aelfric	32.1%	14.3%	39.8%
Cnut	33.4%	12.5%	57.1%
P. Ch. I, II	39.0%	10.0%	26.3%
P. Ch. II:	36.6%	8.5	25.3%
Horn	16.1%	7.0%	31.6%
Piers Plowman	26.4%	23.8%	36.5%
Sermons	11.0%	0.3%	1.1%

ler's study of *Melibeus* and *The Parson's Tale* it follows that Chaucer is somewhere between *Piers Plowman* and *Middle English Sermons*.

The table on p. 107, based on the available statistics, presents the full numerical data.[6]

---

[6] The statistical data are derived from the respective studies mentioned in the Bibliography.

5. CONCLUSION

The study dealt with three aspects of Middle English word order: 1) the relation of subject to predicate, 2) the relation of predicate to the other elements in the clause, 3) the position of the object.

The three versions of *Piers Plowman* were treated as a whole, because they exhibit the same characteristics with only slight differences in degree; in none of the texts are all the analysed features represented to the highest degree. *Middle English Sermons* were studied separately because of some differences in the inventory and the distribution of word order patterns. In both texts, however, the same correlation between word order patterning and semantic load patterns has been found.

It has been established in Chapter 1 that the subject-predicate sequence is typical for both texts (77.6% and 89.0%). The predicate-subject order was found to be determined by the prepositional in a double way: Direct dependence is the result of closeness of syntactical relationship between the prepositional and the predicate (Tables X, XXIX), while the prepositional influences the order indirectly through its semantic load. The test for the predictability of word order patterns on the basis of a known prepositional was negative, but that for the predictability of semantic load patterns was positive (Tables XXIII, XXIV, XXV, XXXIII, XXXIV).

The comparatively few instances of predicate-subject order in non-prepositional sequences are also closely associated with the semantic load patterns. The tendency to a juxtaposition of elements of unequal semantic load (01, 10) is very strong in both word orders, the distribution of typical and non-typical semantic load patterns being nearly identical in the subject-predicate and predicate-subject orders (Table XX). Since this is the case, and since the choice between a pronominal (light) or a nominal (heavy) subject, a light or heavy predicate, as well as a light or heavy prepositional is determined by the objective situation, it is concluded that the user of the language, as represented by the texts, choses one or the other word order to suit the "rhythmic" pattern. In other words, it is maintained that word order patterns depend on semantic load patterns, not the reverse.

The necessary reservation for this conclusion, as well as for those that follow, is the awareness of the limitations dictated by the method adopted in the present study; most certainly word order is correlated with many other factors, which here are disregarded.

In Chapter 2 three positions of the predicate have been distinguished, the most typical being the first place after the subject (52.3% and 97.2%). Medail and final positions occur more frequently in *Piers Plowman* than in the *Sermons*. In both texts the occurrence of clause-final predicates is higher in subordinate than in main clauses. Since in all three positions, the only exception being the final position in the *Sermons,* the predicate forms typical and non-typical semantic load patterns in roughly equal proportions, and since similar proportions are found in other word groups, it seems that the three positinos can be accounted for as providing the possibility for the predicate to find itself in favourable "rhythmic" surroundings. This view is strengthened by the high percentage of typical semantic load patterns in non-typical positions of the predicate, as compared with the typical position.

The inventory as well as the distribution of patterns, which the object forms with the subject and predicate, is somewhat different in *Piers Plowman* and the *Sermons*; in both texts, however, the subject-predicate-object (or the predicate-object) sequence is most typical (83.1% and 91.8%). In this order the object is found in non-typical "rhythmic" surroundings fairly often, while in the other patterns (SXP, XSP, PXS, XPS, XP) it always – or almost always – forms typical semantic load patterns with its neighbours. The same refers to the typical

sequence, when a distinction is made between objects in immediate juxtaposition with their predicates (or subjects) and
those surrounded by other words (SP . . . X, X . . . PS etc.) The
third premise for a conclusion is the very rare occurrence of
non-typical word order in the *Sermons* in a situation, where the
typical word order invariably offers a typical semantic load
pattern to the object. If it is added that the semantic load of
each particular element is determined by the objective situation,
and that the "microscopic" distribution of semantic load patterns
is in agreement with the "macroscopic" distribution, there are
enough reasons for maintaining not only that in subject-predicate-
object relations semantic load patterns are a very important
factor, but also that the presence of the non-typical word order
patterns may be treated as providing the object with a possibility
of finding itself in favourable "rhythmic" surroundings.

SELECTED BIBLIOGRAPHY

I. TEXTS

1. Ross, W. O., (ed.), *Middle English Sermons* (London, Oxford, 1940).
2. Skeat, W. W., (ed.), *The Vision of William Concerning Piers the Plowman. In Three Parallel Texts* (Oxford, 1886).

II. TEXTUAL CRITICISM

3. Bernard, E., *A Grammatical Treatise on the Language of William Langland* (Bonn, 1874).
4. Bloohambers, R. W., "The Three Texts of 'Piers Plowman' and Their Grammatical Forms", *Modern Language Review*, 1919.
5. Chambers, R. W., Grattan, J. G. H., "The Text of Piers Plowman", *Modern Language Review*, XXVI (1931).
6. Donaldson, E. T., *Piers Plowman* (New Haven, 1949).
7. Dunning, A., *Piers Plowman: An Interpretation of the A-Text* (London, 1937).
8. Fowler, D. C., "The Relationship of the Three Texts of Piers Plowman", *Modern Philology*, L (1952).
9. Kittner, F., *Studien zum Wortschatz William Langlands* (Halle, 1937).
10. Korn, R., *William Langleys Buch von Peter dem Pflüger. Untersuchungen über das Handschriftenverhältnis und den Dialekt* (Göttingen, 1886).
11. Teichmann, E., *Die Verbalflexion in William Langley's Buche von Peter dem Pflüger* (Aachen, 1887).
12. Wandschneider, W., *Zur Syntax des Verbs in Langleys Vision of William Concerning Piers Plowman* (Kiel, 1887).

III. WORD ORDER

13. Andrew, S. O., "Some Principles of Old English Word-Order", *Medium Aevum*, III (1934).
14. Andrew, S. O., *Syntax and Style in Old English* (Cambridge, 1940).
15. Azzalino, W., *Die wortstellung im King Horn* (Halle, 1915).
16. Barrett, C. R., *Studies in the Word-Order of Aelfric's Catholic Homilies and Lives of the Saints* (Cambridge, 1953).

17. Bernecker, H., "Die Wortfolge in den slavischen Sprachen", *Indo-Germanische Forschungen*, XIV (1942).
18. Bernstein, S., *The Order of Words in Old Norse Prose* (Columbia, 1898).
19. Besuch, A., *Studien zur Wortstellung im Alt- und Mittelenglischen* (Breslau, 1903).
20. Borst, E., "Zur Stellung des Adverbs bei Chauser", *Englische Studien*, XLII (1910).
21. Dahlstedt, A., *Word-Order in the Ancren Riwle* (Sundsvall, 1903).
22. Eitle, H., *Die satzverknüpfung bei Chauser* (Kiel, 1914).
23. Henningsen, H. G., *Uber die Worstellung in den Prosaschriften Richard Rolles von Hampole* (Kiel, 1912).
24. Heussler, F., *Die Stellung von Subjekt und Prädikat in den Erzählungen des Melibeus und des Pfarrers in Chaucer's Canterbury Tales* (Wesel, 1888).
25. Jacobsson, B., *Inversion in English with special reference to the Early Modern Enlish Period* (Uppsala, 1951).
26. Klemensiewicz, Z., "Lokalizacja podmiotu i orzeczenia w zdaniach izolowanych", *Biuletyn Polskiego Towarzystwa Jezyk*, IX 1949).
27. Koppitz, A., "Zur gotischen Wortstellung", *Zeitschrift für deutsche Philologie*, XXXII, XXXIII.
28. Kreikemeier, H., *Die Wortstellung im Nebensatz des Englischen* (Giessen, 1915).
29. Laeseke, B., *Ein Beitrag zur Stellung des Verbums im Orrmulum* (Berlin, 1917).
30. McKnight, G. H., "The Primitive Teutonic Order of Words", *Jounal of Germanic Philology*, I (1897).
31. Mueller, P., *Studien zur Altgermanischen Wortstellung* (Berlin, 1930).
32. Ries, J., *Die Stellung von Subject und Prädikativsverbum in Heliand* (Strassburg, 1880).
33. Ries, J., *Die Wortstellung im Beowulf* (Halle, 1907).
34. Rothstein, R., *Wortstellung in der Peterborough Chronicle* (Halle, 1922).
35. Smith, C., *The Order of Words in Anglo-Saxon Prose* (Baltimore, 1893).
36. Snoek, H., *Die wortstellung bei Bunyan* (Marburg, 1902).
37. Szober, S., "Zasady układu wyrazów w zdaniu polskim", *Sprawozdania N.T.W.*, 1933.

IV. GENERAL

38. Herdan, G., *Language As Choice and Chance* (Groningen, 1956).
39. Jespersen, O., *Progress in Language* (New York, 1894).
40. Mirowicz, A., "Z zagadnień struktury Zdania", *Biuletyn Polskiego Towarzystwa Jezykozn.*, IX (1949).

41. Owst, G. R., *Literature and Pulpit of Medieval England* (Cambridge, 1933).
42. Owst, G. R., *Preaching in Medieval England* (Cambridge, 1926).
43. Sapir, E., *Language* (New York).
44. Sweet, H., *A Primer of Spoken English* (Oxford, 1890).

JANUA LINGUARUM

STUDIA MEMORIAE NICOLAI VAN WIJK DEDICATA

Edited by Cornelis H. van Schooneveld

SERIES MINOR